One could not find a more ti
Brave Enough to Believe by Pa.... ...g... ...
father, veteran Pastor Hubert Morris, is an inspiring study of
the apostle Thomas—historically remembered as "doubting
Thomas." The authors explore the disciple's life through the
New Testament narrative and three less-remembered but pivotal
encounters he had with Jesus. Through Thomas's journey
with Jesus and stories from the authors' ministry journeys, we
are reminded that sincere skeptics can also be fervent seekers,
sold-out followers, and seasoned leaders. They can even impact
nations. *Brave Enough to Believe* is a faith-building read for
Jesus-followers and ministry leaders in challenging times. And
it's a needed reminder to allow our hardest questions of faith to
drive us closer to Him, not further away. A welcomed read!

—Dr. Beth Grant,
executive director, Project Rescue;
executive presbyter, Assemblies of God

Thank you, Hubert and Angela, for reminding us that
disappointments don't have to define us and doubt doesn't have
to paralyze us. As you journey through *Brave Enough to Believe*,
you will be encouraged and taught how to starve your doubts and
feed your faith.

—Doug Clay, general superintendent,
General Council of the Assemblies of God

As a lifelong student of the Bible and a relentless pursuer of
truth, I have often found myself being drawn to the men and
women who knew Jesus in the flesh. I have longed to know
what it was like to laugh with Jesus, hear His stirring stories,
and watch in disbelief and awe as He healed the sick and raised
the dead.

I have found a source of Bible treasure in *Brave Enough
to Believe*. In this book, I have felt the sweat of Thomas as he

wrestled with the truth of the ages; I have heard his uneven breathing as he wondered if he was losing his mind.

Brave Enough to Believe combines Bible scholarship with a riveting human-interest story found on the sacred pages of scripture. Reverend Angela Donadio and her father, Reverend Hubert Morris, have combined their years of ministry, communication, and love of the Bible in this one volume that is both earnest study and heartfelt insight.

Brave Enough to Believe is for two types of readers: those who love to study the Bible and those who wonder if their doubts are too massive to overcome. I believe that we all fit into both categories.

Although this is their first book written together, I certainly hope that it won't be their last!

—Carol McLeod,
Bible teacher and best-selling author,
podcaster, and blogger

Angela Donadio and her father Rev. Hubert Morris have done something unusually effective: they have coauthored a book that reads seamlessly. This study of the life of the apostle Thomas, as in "Doubting Thomas," provides an engaging study of this disciple within the context of Jesus' ministry as described in the four Gospels. Each chapter concludes with Angela and her dad's particular testimonies and insights about Thomas and what it means to follow Jesus. I truly enjoyed reading this book and endorse it without reservation! It is well worth your time to read and digest.

—Dr. Doug Beacham,
general superintendent,
International Pentecostal Holiness Church

It was my distinct privilege to work with Pastor Hubert Morris for several years in local church ministry. He and his daughter, Pastor

Angela Donadio, have now given us a wonderful gift in their new book on the life of Thomas, *Brave Enough to Believe*. I found it an insightful and inspiring read—refreshingly honest and personally faith-building. It narrates the story of Jesus' profound influence on the apostle Thomas, leaving Thomas to grapple in unexpected ways with who Jesus was and what spiritual growth could look like. At a time when so many are struggling to make sense of the world around them, including their own faith, this book is a word in season for every one of us.

—Dr. James Bradford, Senior Pastor,
Central Assembly of God, Springfield, Missouri;
former General Secretary of the General
Council of the Assemblies of God

Brave Enough to Believe is a book of insight and life-changing revelations. You will never see Thomas, Jesus, or yourself the same way again! Pastor Angela and her father take you on a journey into the heart of God. You'll come face-to-face with your own doubts and insecurities only to find a fresh faith in a compassionate Jesus. As a missionary in India, I pondered the life of Thomas many times. I was intrigued by how he overcame his fear of the unknown yet walked in unshakable faith. How in the midst of persecution he was brave enough to believe God would use him to bring light to a dark continent. This book is a treasure trove of faith, hope, and how to face your doubts and fulfill your call! God is with you! Be brave enough to believe!

—Susanne Cox, founder of Legacy of Purpose

In *Brave Enough to Believe*, Pastors Hubert Morris and Angela Donadio teach us how to move from seeing in order to believe to believing even though we have not seen. I have stood at the grave of apostle Thomas in Chennai, India. Even though Thomas is known for his doubting, he went further than any other New Testament apostle in carrying the gospel to unreached people.

This remarkable book will equip you to fight the good fight of faith and to finish the race that the Lord has marked out for you!

—Dr. James O. Davis,
founder/president, Global Church Network

It's easy to believe our doubts and doubt our beliefs when circumstances spin out of control. This book provides a powerful reset to stand firm in faith, move forward resolutely, and reclaim your purpose in your generation. We all need a resource to show us how wrestling through doubt serves to embolden and empower us and this book is it! It's time to stop allowing our doubts to define, derail, and deconstruct our foundations of faith. This book is a road map to unshakable faith.

—Erica Wiggenhorn,
author of *Letting God Be Enough* and
An Unexpected Revival

Brave Enough to Believe is a NOW word for the body of Christ! If we're honest, we've all had our "Thomas moments" during the protracted battle in which we've lived. Do like I did: grab your Bible, notebook, and *Brave Enough to Believe* and take a personal retreat with God. Give God the time and space to encounter you afresh, like He did Thomas, to bolster your faith and heal your heart.

—Rev. Dr. Jamie Morgan,
pastor, author, podcaster, mentor

BRAVE ENOUGH TO BELIEVE

HOW *the life of* DOUBTING THOMAS ANSWERS *our hard* QUESTIONS

ANGELA DONADIO *with her father*, HUBERT MORRIS

IRON STREAM

Birmingham, Alabama

Brave Enough to Believe

An imprint of Iron Stream Media
100 Missionary Ridge
Birmingham, AL 35242
IronStreamMedia.com

Library of Congress Control Number: 2022939448

ISBN: 978-1-56309-611-2 (paperback)
ISBN: 978-1-56309-612-9 (e-book)

1 2 3 4 5—27 26 25 24 23

Reverend Angela Donadio
To Dale, my husband and partner for life. Your love steadies
me through every adventure. Your support both personally
and theologically is unparalleled, and I'm forever grateful. To
Gabrielle and Christian, I pray that the words in this book
from your Grandpa and Mom encourage you to stay brave
enough to believe in Jesus no matter what.

Reverend Hubert Morris
To the love of my life, Glenda Shows Morris, my faithful
partner in life. I would not be the man I am today without
your love and support. I am so proud to have you by my side.

Contents

Foreword

When I learned authors Hubert Morris and Angela Donadio were writing a book together, I said, "That's one book I'm going to purchase." I'm especially drawn to books authored by people who are motivated by the right things, practice what they preach, and have something important to say. Hubert Morris and Angela and their book, *Brave Enough to Believe*, check all three boxes.

I have known Hubert and his wife, Glenda, for forty years. Glenda served as my administrative assistant and Hubert ministered at my mother's funeral. The Morrises have served faithfully as pastors for many years, where they earned a reputation for kindness and compassion. Hubert has also been active in world missions, sharing the message of Jesus in places like China, Sri Lanka, Haiti, and more. In addition, he spearheaded several Convoy of Hope citywide outreaches to meet the needs of hurting people in the community where he pastored.

Angela (Morris) Donadio shares her parents' love for God's Word and their heart for people. She has served alongside her husband, Dale, in pastoral ministry for three decades. Her Bible studies, podcasts, and speaking have ministered to women around the world. Her advocacy work with women in Africa only further expresses her commitment to kingdom purpose.

Through *Brave Enough to Believe*, the authors demonstrate their admiration for those who followed Jesus at all costs and demonstrated compassion to people bruised by doubt and uncertainty. This book comes at a time when untold millions have experienced isolation, heartache, and pain from an unwanted pandemic. By exploring the life of the apostle Thomas, the authors provide a road map from uncertainty to resolute faith. They chronicle how one ordinary man became a world-changer and how he was transformed by an encounter with Jesus Christ.

Thomas resembles many today who seek answers to life's greatest questions. I'm confident *Brave Enough to Believe* will introduce you to a Thomas you didn't know and help you discover answers to your own questions. Just as Jesus drew Thomas out of the shadows of isolation and despair, this book is an invitation to a life of uncompromising faith and unparalleled purpose.

Hal Donaldson
founder/CEO
Convoy of Hope

CHAPTER 1

An Ache for More

Doubting Thomas.

Chances are, you've heard or even used this two-word phrase at some point in your life. To trace the origins of this common expression, you'll need to journey through the ancient texts of the Bible and meet a man named Thomas. Perhaps you know Thomas for his bouts with doubt, but Jesus knew Thomas for the courage to question and the bravery to believe. When a crisis of faith revealed his deepest doubts, Jesus met his deepest longings. Thomas left behind uncertainty for a life of unwavering faith. And when we personally encounter Jesus, we can too.

Thomas experienced four major encounters with Jesus that defined the trajectory of his life. As we walk in his dusty footsteps, we will witness how each one shaped Thomas into a man brave enough to believe Jesus and follow Him at all costs. Brave resilience isn't relegated only to a select group of spiritual giants or biblical heroes—it's offered to us as well.

We crave the courage to stand firm in a culture rocked by upheaval. Amid a global pandemic, civil unrest, financial instability, and the strained sinews of relationships, the nagging ache of uncertainty commanded center stage. Disruption is disorienting. Shaken by fear, isolation, and loss, many of us grew weary and afraid to hope. Despite a barrage of information and opinions, we were left with more questions than answers, unsure of who or what to believe.

The bitter soil of unmet expectations provides the breeding ground for disappointment—and disappointment bruises the bravest of souls. It clothes itself in many ways. Sometimes disappointment looks like deep hurt caused by something someone did to us or situations beyond our control. Other times, we wear the disappointment we have in ourselves, caused by our mistakes or poor decisions. We may even wonder if our purpose has been taken hostage. Honest reflection reveals the places where our faith becomes dampened by the unknown. What do we do when doubt entices us to wonder if God is good when life is not?

As we examine the life of Thomas, we find a road map that leads us out of the clutches of confusion and into the confidence of faith. Thomas never owned an iPhone. He didn't boast followers on Instagram or host a podcast. He didn't fight the frustration of a morning commute or navigate the challenges of leading in the era of online church.

Although Thomas is a stranger in every way to our modern culture, few people are more qualified to speak to the questions our generation asks today. His story holds the answers we seek.

Perhaps you're wondering where God is in your circumstances or if He cares about what concerns you. Your hard questions are opportunities for God to reveal Himself to you. He created you with an insatiable desire to know Him and be known by Him. Within the pages of Scripture, you're invited to meet the God that transforms the ache of uncertainty into the ache for more of Him. He won't leave you in a place of spiritual hunger. He will fill you with His presence, His power, and His promises for every situation. You were designed for a life of expectation and action.

You can be brave enough to believe.

Where It Began for Thomas

Who was this "Doubting Thomas"? Scripture also refers to him as Didymus, meaning twin or two sides. Perhaps he had a twin brother. Or this may indicate his need to investigate all sides of an issue before committing himself to it. Although the Gospels of Matthew, Mark, Luke, and John do not provide a detailed backstory, we know Thomas, a Jew, hailed from the region of Galilee. Growing up in Jewish homes, children like Thomas learned the stories contained in the Old Testament and the miracles God's people experienced throughout history. They heard about men like David who defeated Israel's enemies and honored God's presence. They knew about women like Esther, who risked her life to save her people from annihilation.

Most important, they heard about the Messiah who was to come. They believed the promised Messiah would bring salvation from sin and relief from the oppressive rule of the Roman government. Thomas ached for more than his current circumstances; he longed for a deliverer.

We are first introduced to Thomas as one of the crowd present in the early stages of Jesus's ministry. Matthew 4:23–25 shares:

> Jesus went throughout Galilee, teaching in their synagogues, proclaiming the good news of the kingdom, and healing every disease and sickness among the people. News about him spread all over Syria, and people brought to him all who were ill with various diseases, those suffering severe pain, the demon-possessed, those having seizures, and the paralyzed; and he healed them. Large crowds from Galilee, the Decapolis, Jerusalem, Judea and the region across the Jordan followed him.

Word about Jesus traveled everywhere. Thomas listened intently as his neighbors shared their stories. It seemed inexplicable. But right in front of him stood the evidence: blind eyes could see, paralyzed legs could move, tormented minds could once again think clearly. Friends were freed from their suffering when nothing else helped. More than just healings, Jesus taught in the synagogues with authority and power. He preached in the open about the kingdom of God. Hearing the news that Jesus taught nearby, Thomas resolved that no matter what it took, he needed to see Jesus for himself. At that time in Israel, a traveling public speaker would sometimes use a hillside as an amphitheater. Drawn by a curious mind, an investigative spirit, and a thirsty soul, Thomas took his seat among the expectant crowd.

He showed up as a seeker and considered whether or not to follow Jesus. Not only did he want to hear from this teacher, but Thomas also wanted to know that he heard the truth. Filled with questions, he thought Jesus might be the answer. The air on the mountain grew thick with excitement as those in the crowd waited with anticipation. *Jesus was here.* A new day dawned unlike any they had experienced before.

Matthew 5:1–2 says, "Now when Jesus saw the crowds, he went up on a mountainside and sat down. His disciples came to him, and he began to teach them." The Gospel of Matthew, chapters 5–7, contains many principles for living out the kingdom of God on the earth. In the "Sermon on the Mount," Jesus shared The Beatitudes, blessings for our lives. Thomas listened and sensed something different about Jesus.

Jesus spoke of a loving and kind God who wanted people to be blessed. He described the way we should live, love our enemies, give to the needy, and pray. He offered guidance about what to do with worry and anxiety and cautioned about our propensity to judge others. He taught what it means to be a true disciple and implored all to seek the kingdom above all else. Thomas hung on His every word.

Blessed are the poor in spirit,
>   for theirs is the kingdom of heaven.
Blessed are those who mourn,
>   for they will be comforted.
Blessed are the meek,
>   for they will inherit the earth.
Blessed are those who hunger and thirst for
righteousness,
>   for they will be filled.
Blessed are the merciful,
>   for they will be shown mercy.
Blessed are the pure in heart,
>   for they will see God.
Blessed are the peacemakers,
>   for they will be called children of God.
Blessed are those who are persecuted because of
righteousness,
>   for theirs is the kingdom of heaven.

Blessed are you when people insult you, persecute you and falsely say all kinds of evil against you because of me. Rejoice and be glad, because great is your reward in heaven, for in the same way they persecuted the prophets who were before you. (Matthew 5:3–12)

Thomas's thoughts raced. *I hunger and thirst for righteousness. . . . I want to know and see God. . . . I want to know how to inherit the kingdom of God. . . . I **have** to know. I've heard many voices of opinion and yet nothing satisfies. I'm so tired of feeling uncertain. I want to believe that Jesus has the answers I'm looking for. Can I truly trust Him?*

"When Jesus had finished saying these things, the crowds were amazed at his teaching, because he taught as one who had authority, and not as the teachers of the law [of Moses]" (Matthew 7:28–29).

As Thomas heard Jesus teach, he began to gain the confidence to trust Jesus for more. Earnest and desperate, something within

5

him would not be content until he got closer to this teacher called Jesus. We will see that Jesus called him out of the crowd to answer his deep soul ache and use him greatly in the kingdom. It all started because Thomas chose to show up. Thomas became one of those disciples, "followers of Jesus," ready to be taught by Him.

Perhaps, like Thomas, you just found your way to the back of a crowd, unsure about who Jesus is. Your ache for more can either drive you to Jesus or away from Him. When you allow it to lead you closer to Jesus, faith can overcome your fear. If you've never accepted Jesus Christ as your personal Savior, you can start your journey with this simple prayer: *Jesus, I know I am a sinner. I believe You are the Son of God. I believe You died on the cross for my sins and rose again. I ask You to forgive my sins and become Lord of my life. Amen.*

Our Starting Place Is Not Our Staying Place

When we enter into a relationship with Jesus, we grow in relationship with other believers. Following a worldwide pandemic, many drifted apart from a sense of community. For some, the chasm of uncertainty turned into a cavernous separation from friends, coworkers, and even family. However, we don't have to stay in the shadows. It's time to step out of the catacombs of isolation and into community with those choosing faith in Jesus Christ. We can replace isolation by association with other followers of Jesus.

Thomas did exactly that. He followed Jesus down the mountain, and his faith in Jesus grew as he witnessed the miraculous:

- Jesus invaded the territory where demons had been holding people captive and delivered a man from an evil spirit. Jesus told the evil spirits to leave and they obeyed. Thomas had never seen anything like it.

- Jesus went to the home of a disciple, Peter, where his mother-in-law lay ill. He healed her in an instant. The whole town gathered at her door, and Jesus healed many who were sick and demon-possessed into the late hours of the night.
- Men brought a paralyzed man to Jesus but could not get through the crowd. Thomas watched in amazement as the man's friends cut a hole in the roof and lowered the man down to Jesus. Before healing the man, Thomas heard Jesus say with authority, "Your sins are forgiven."

Thomas stood in awe at the compassion Jesus demonstrated for those who were suffering, Jesus healed on the Sabbath, cleansed the lepers, and touched the outcasts of society. Thomas observed the obvious distinction between what he knew of the law and the rabbis of the day versus what he saw and heard from this new teacher.

Jesus separates Himself from the teachings of the world, of shifting cultures and world philosophies. He is unlike the leaders of man-made religions who offer only the relentless pursuit of our works to free ourselves from the guilt and sin that separates us from God. But man-made mechanisms are only a mirage; they cannot save. In our ache for a way to make things right, we can exhaust ourselves trying to find freedom. We can tether our hope to other sources of security rather than fully trust in God. It's not enough to simply be a seeker of truth; we must go to the source of truth just as Thomas did. Only Jesus has the power and authority to forgive sin.

Jesus had authority from the beginning of the creation of the universe. John 1:1–2 says, "In the beginning was the Word, and the Word was with God, and the Word was God. He was with God in the beginning." He continues in verse 14, "The Word became flesh and made his dwelling among us. We have seen his glory, the glory of the one and only Son, who came from the Father, full of grace and truth."

Jesus is fully God. The Bible also tells us that Jesus is the beginning and the end, the same yesterday, today, and forever. Although life may be uncertain, His character is unchanging. He alone is worthy of our faith and devotion. We can trade our uncertainty for confidence in His authority. He transforms painful experiences into opportunities to grow closer to Him. He empowers us to lead bravely through every season of life.

This book guides us through the four major encounters between Thomas and Jesus. As we explore them, we will find answers to many of the questions that we are asking today.

- How do I hear from God?
- What do I do with my doubts?
- What do I need to know about Jesus to fully trust Him?
- Is Jesus the only way to heaven?
- How can I be sure I'm going to heaven when I die?
- How do I get untangled from uncertainty and cope with it in godly ways?
- How can I know my purpose and the ways God wants to use me in my generation?
- What are the barriers to bravery and how do I remove them?
- How do I leverage adversity?
- What will help me follow Jesus well and lead with confidence?

Friend, we are embarking on a journey not just to know Thomas or the answers we seek. We will know ourselves more authentically and the God who loves us more intimately. We want to provide you with tools to get, and stay, unstuck from places of pain that are driving you away from God. We want to walk with you as you process your hard questions through the filter of His goodness. It is possible to feel steady in the face of uncertainty and recover your peace in the midst of overwhelm.

Disappointment can be the catalyst not for spiritual apostasy but for spiritual awakening.

No matter where you are in your faith journey—a seeker, skeptic, or seasoned leader—Jesus invites you to be brave enough to believe in Him and to stand up for what you believe. The story of Thomas will help you know how to live untangled from uncertainty and awakened to purpose. You will discover ways to leverage adversity as an opportunity for unparalleled spiritual growth. You will gain the ability to lead with confidence through challenging circumstances. In writing this book, our highest goal is for you to find yourself following Thomas into a life you never dreamed of before—a life of tenacious faith.

A Dad and Daughter's Perspectives

As coauthors of this book, we wrote every chapter together through the gift of Google docs, face-to-face meetings, and hundreds of hours of phone calls. We also included sections designated as "Up Close" narratives in our own words. We have shared our individual life experiences from a combined eighty-plus years of ministry. We loved every moment of writing this book and praying over you. We believe you will encounter God in a fresh way through the life of Thomas.

Up Close with Angela

The concept for this book first came to me in November of 2020 while my husband, Dale, and I regrouped for a few days at a friend's beach house in Outer Banks, North Carolina. Most of us found ourselves in the clutches of COVID-19, a political firestorm, and unfamiliar terrain. Despite thirty years of full-time ministry, I struggled to see God's hand at work in the middle of it all. I would identify myself as a sold-out follower and a seasoned leader, yet, uncertainty and adversity uncovered areas where I also identified as a seeker and a skeptic. Intellectually, I knew God as present, sovereign, and good. Emotionally, however, I fought to manage the tension between doubt and faith—and I knew I wasn't alone.

Perhaps there is no better setting to process unsettled thoughts and unruly emotions than in view of the ocean. I stared at the expanse of sky and sea and reflected back over the unexpected challenges in previous months that crashed over us like the breaking waves. In addition to a global and national crisis, I spent the year healing from injuries sustained in a car accident. As I made my way through a green light at forty-five miles per hour, another driver failed to yield. I blacked out on impact, crossed a lane of traffic, and regained consciousness on a curb. The airbag deployed, and in the aftermath, my car filled with the purple haze of smoke. I sustained injuries to both hands and wrists, warranting a cast on my right, dominant hand, and two surgeries on the left. A severe concussion and whiplash proved a formidable nemesis requiring a variety of approaches to stem debilitating headaches for months to come.

A survivor of two near-death health crises in 2001 and 2003, I'm no stranger to adversity. I added new scars to my collection, ones I can easily see on my hand and wrist. They, like the others, become remembrances, not of simply a dark season but of the God who is our refuge. He promises purpose out of pain.

Somehow, the compound effect of a painful recovery on top of all 2020 asked of us tested my faith in new ways. As pastors of River of Life Church in Virginia, Dale and I navigated the unprecedented demands of providing the best possible online church experience in the wake of a national shutdown. Only weeks after reopening, Dale and several of our staff became ill with COVID-19, some requiring hospitalization. We moved forward a second time with the unique dynamic of reduced crowds and social distancing. Our hearts ached for teachers and parents struggling with online learning and working from home, for healthcare workers depleted from long hours and brutal demands, and for our overseas church plants we couldn't visit.

Above everything, we ached for more of God. We emerged with greater dependency than ever on the Holy Spirit. The pain of a crisis simply reveals what's underneath that needs work. Issues and inconveniences spotlight what needs recalibration in God's presence and a reset in God's Word.

So, back to the beach. I wrote this in my journal: "We all have them. Sometimes we just think them. We don't want anyone to hear us say it out loud. That tucked away, in silent spaces, we have doubts. Other times, we scream it—loud so all the world can hear. God, are You good? Are You who You say You are? Where are You in this?"

As I walked the sandy shores, I called my dad and shared some of my thoughts with him. My dad is my hero in the faith. He and my mom instilled in me the love I have for the Word of God. My internal journey in my quiet times with God had been leading me to the life of Thomas. I didn't know that God laid Thomas on my dad's heart as well. As we talked, God began to deposit revelations that would become the book you now hold in your hands.

This is the book I needed to read. I addressed my own difficult questions. In Thomas, I found a travel companion and a trusted friend who leads us to a life of tenacious faith. My prayer is that within these pages, you come close enough to Jesus to leave behind uncertainty and find the bravery to believe.

Up Close with Hubert

I felt deep joy and honor when my daughter Angela suggested that we coauthor this book together. My wife, Glenda, and I have raised three daughters who are women of faith in Jesus Christ. They have seen Jesus at work in their lives when faced with decisions and opportunities.

Throughout fifty-plus years in full-time Christian ministry, I have witnessed countless people have their doubts removed as the power of Christ's love and His presence brought the answers they needed. Faith, certainty, and confidence in God is a beautiful thing. I have seen it happen with people in the churches where I led as pastor, with college students where I served as a vice president of Evangel University in Springfield, Missouri, and with the six hundred senior adults where I ministered as care pastor.

I had an experience that involved "doubting Thomas" when my wife and I took a trip to Fresno, California, in the fall of 2019. We spent a few days with our granddaughter and her husband and attended their church on a Sunday morning. When we walked into the church foyer at Mountain View Community Church, I saw a painting of the apostle Thomas hanging there. I studied it for a moment and my mouth must have fallen open. The artist portrayed Jesus taking hold of Thomas's arm, pulling Thomas closer to Himself, inviting Thomas to put his finger into the wound in Jesus's side. I could not hold back the tears. That experience made me want to share the story of Thomas and Jesus.

The portrayal of the resurrected Son of God doing whatever it took to bring Thomas to life-changing faith impressed me about Jesus in a deeper way. Jesus did all Thomas needed to restore his faith and his devotion to Him. Thomas would never again wonder about the resurrection power of Jesus Christ and the divinity of Jesus Christ, the Son of God. I shared with Angela my experience concerning the painting of Thomas and Jesus. This confirmed in her heart that we should write this book together.

During my years of ministry, I have witnessed Jesus doing all that it took to restore faith to many people who were filled with doubts. This book is written with the hope and the belief that the story of Thomas will make your faith stronger and fortify you to face the uncertainties of the future. Like Thomas, you may simply need a fresh encounter with Jesus that makes you brave enough to believe Him and to stand up for Him.

You will need bravery and confidence in Jesus Christ to face continuing upheaval and conflict on the earth. You will encounter adversity. This book will help you not only face it but leverage it for your own spiritual growth and the encouragement of others. You will be built up in your prayer life and your emotions and strengthened to face any attack by Satan and his emissaries. God will prove Himself faithful to you, just as He did with Thomas.

Come Closer

Takeaway
Our starting place is not our staying place.

Friend, we are embarking on a journey, not just to know Thomas or the answers we seek. We will know ourselves more authentically and the God who loves us more intimately. As we begin, these chapter reviews and three questions will help you identify your starting place.

1. Thomas showed up as a seeker and considered whether or not to follow Jesus.
Would you characterize yourself as a seeker, skeptic, sold-out follower, or seasoned leader?

2. Within the pages of Scripture, you're invited to meet the God that transforms the ache of uncertainty into the ache for more of Him. He won't leave you in a place of spiritual hunger. He will fill you with His presence, His power, and His promises for every situation. You were designed for a life of expectation and action.
What is one way you want to grow in brave faith as you study the life of Thomas?

3. As we explore the four major encounters between Thomas and Jesus, we will find answers to many of the questions that we are asking today.

Which of the ten questions we listed in chapter 1 do you most need answered at this point in your life?

ENCOUNTER 1

CHAPTER 2

Called Out of the Crowd

Scripture is replete with God encounters, moments where God called ordinary men and women to do extraordinary things. For some, the call came through a dramatic event. Moses heard God speak to him from a burning bush in a desert. Mary received a divine assignment from an angelic messenger that she would give birth to the Messiah. Saul fell to the ground while on a journey to persecute believers in Damascus, blinded by a bright light and accosted by the voice of Jesus.

Others experienced God speaking to them in quiet and understated ways, although no less meaningful. Elijah waited on the side of a mountain through a windstorm, an earthquake, and fire to discern the gentle whisper of God. Nicodemus met Jesus privately under the cover of darkness to understand what it meant to be born again. Thomas heard Jesus call him out of the crowd to become an apostle, not amid fanfare and spectacle, but from a solitary place of prayer.

> One of those days Jesus went out to a mountainside to pray, and spent the night praying to God. When morning came, he called his disciples to him and chose twelve of them, whom he also designated apostles: Simon (whom he named Peter), his brother Andrew, James, John, Philip, Bartholomew, Matthew, Thomas, James son of Alphaeus, Simon who was called the Zealot, Judas son of James, and Judas Iscariot, who became a traitor. (Luke 6:12–16)

This pivotal moment began the first of four recorded encounters between Thomas and Jesus. He received the confirmation from his Heavenly Father to choose Thomas and the other eleven apostles after a full night spent in prayer. An *apostle* is defined as "a sent one with a special commission," "an authorized agent/representative."[1] This signified the distinct purpose God planned for the life of Thomas.

Thomas's call to become an apostle constituted a far greater commitment than simply that of a listener in a crowd. He bravely left the comfort and security of all he knew to embrace the mission of Jesus. He entered a season of preparation as Jesus sought to help the apostles truly understand His mission so they could be an extension of His hands. They filled a unique role in the foundation of the church after Jesus's death and resurrection. In the next chapter, we will travel with Thomas to see how Jesus sent the apostles out to minister on their own. First, let's examine some of the ways we know to fulfill the call of God in our lives.

Start with Prayer

Jesus placed a high value on prayer, evidenced in the way prayer preceded the call of Thomas. Jesus placed top priority on His unity with the Father. He often found solitary places to pray to His Father at length before He made decisions. When Thomas and the apostles witnessed Jesus's commitment to prayer, they asked Him to teach them how to pray. He answered them with what we call, "The Lord's Prayer." He modeled this pattern of prayer for His apostles and for us.

Matthew 6:9–15 says,

This, then, is how you should pray:
"Our Father in heaven,
hallowed be your name,
your kingdom come,
your will be done,
    on earth as it is in heaven.
Give us today our daily bread.
And forgive us our debts,
    as we also have forgiven our debtors.
And lead us not into temptation,
    but deliver us from the evil one."

For if you forgive other people when they sin against you, your heavenly Father will also forgive you. But if you do not forgive others their sins, your Father will not forgive your sins.

We learn much from Jesus in this passage. If He needed to pray, how much more do we need to spend time in prayer. This is a primary way we become untangled from uncertainty and hear from God. Prayer is a conversation that starts with a vertical focus as we align our heart and will with the Father. Jesus began with an emphasis on "our" Father, not just My Father. He takes us with Him into the presence of the Father when He intercedes for us in prayer. When we pray to our Father, we start with a mindset that includes and values relationships with others. The Father's name is to be hallowed or reverenced in prayer. When we honor Him in this way, He releases power to accomplish His will. In Jesus's example, we see how to submit our will to the Father and invite His Kingdom to reign on the earth and in our hearts.

Jesus transitioned from an upward focus to an inward focus. Through prayer, we acknowledge our dependence on God for daily provision for our earthly needs. We ask for forgiveness for our sins and for the grace to forgive others. We receive deliverance from any temptation that threatens to derail God's call on our lives, empowering us to live in victory.

We can only imagine what it was like for Thomas to learn from Jesus face-to-face . . . to look Him in the eyes as He taught . . . to walk with Him through village streets and watch Him heal. However, we can get to know Jesus intimately and personally through His Word and through our time in prayer with Him. Prayer is the life-giving force in our relationship with God as we communicate with Him.

Prayer preceded the ministry of Jesus and His apostles. We cannot overstate the importance of prayer as we seek to encounter God and do what He calls us to do. Oswald Chambers said, "Prayer does not equip us for greater works—prayer *is* the greater work."[2] We strengthen the potency of our prayer life as we train our ear to listen for God's voice. Allow for times of silence and reflection during prayer, not to empty our mind, but to quiet it so God can renew it. We can implement the same valuable keys Jesus taught Thomas as we learn to listen well:

- Find a solitary place to pray.
- Free yourself from distraction.
- Frame your situation with the truth of God's Word.

Prayer prepares our hearts to receive guidance just as Jesus received confirmation from His Father throughout His ministry. God gives us direction and clarity in several ways. First, we can read a passage of Scripture that seems to leap off the page as the Holy Spirit illuminates it. At times, we may receive confirmation of an answer when circumstances align in a way that only God could have made possible. Even still, God may close a door and give us the peace we need to trust that we are in the center of His will. **Outcomes originate in prayer.** Author and leadership expert Jessie Seneca states, "Obedience is up to you. The outcome is up to God."[3]

As we devote ourselves to prayer and His word, Jesus leads us from a starting place to a sending place. Just as He spent time preparing Thomas and the other apostles, He prepares us before He sends us. When we start in the crowd, we may find safety in numbers. The crowd may allow us to stay anonymous and unchallenged. The crowd is noisy and full of distractions. However, as we move closer to Jesus through prayer and relationship, we grow in our identity in Him and our influence with others. We impact our culture *for* Jesus when we're close enough to Him to be taught and changed *by* Jesus. This leads to the successful fulfillment of the individual call of God upon our lives.

Called by God

Although we are not one of the twelve apostles, we have much in common with Thomas. We are called first to salvation and then to service. You are known, loved, and chosen by God to make a difference in the lives of others. First Peter 2:9 says, "But you are a chosen people, a royal priesthood, a holy nation, God's special possession, that you may declare the praises of him who called you out of the darkness into his wonderful light." Let's explore the way this verse frames our calling.

First, God calls each of us out of darkness and into the light of His salvation and grace. We are confronted with the choice to accept Jesus, forsake our sin, and receive His forgiveness. This call may come from reading or hearing God's Word, from a sermon, or through the testimony of another believer. Jesus also calls people to Himself through dreams, encounters, and miracles. When we accept Him in faith, He forgives us and dwells in us through the Holy Spirit. With this brave step, we begin a new life, transformed by the love and mercy of God.

Second, God calls us into a relationship with Him as His very own possession. He knows us intimately and calls us by name, just as He did with Thomas. As image bearers of God, we learn His character which helps us to discern His voice. John records the words of Jesus in John 10:27: "My sheep listen to my voice; I know them, and they follow me." Three voices vie for our attention: God's, Satan's, and our own. How do we know the difference?

God's voice will never contradict His written Word. At times, we may need other believers to help us filter what we believe we are hearing from God. We avoid error and stay in agreement with God's will when we confirm that a decision aligns with the Bible. God can speak to us through our conscience to lead us away from evil and into His will. We may sense His audible voice within our mind and inner spirit. Even when the heavens seem silent, don't allow doubt to choke out the confidence that God hears and answers. These seasons serve to deepen our faith as we depend fully on the grace of God and His written Word as our final authority.

The second voice we hear is that of the Enemy. Satan seeks to condemn, while the Holy Spirit seeks to convict. Conviction is rooted in love. Condemnation is rooted in shame. Although they both cause us to grieve, conviction is hopeful, but condemnation leads to hopelessness. James 4:7 gives us steps we can take to negate the voice of the Enemy. "Submit yourselves, then, to God. Resist the devil, and he will flee from you." Don't engage in dialogue with the Enemy or let him intimidate you. Trust God to direct you; He is greater.

The voice we most often hear is our own—and it is loud. We may experience times of uncertainty as we try to distinguish God's voice from our own. Pastor Mark Ballenger puts it this way: "Your voice serves you. God's voice serves God."[4] Our selfish motives can easily muddy the waters of decision. We gain clarity as we wait on God and gather any pertinent information. Philippians 4:6–7 tells us what to do in these situations: "Do not be anxious about anything, but in every situation, by prayer and petition, with thanksgiving, present your requests to God. And the peace of God, which transcends all understanding, will guard your hearts and your minds in Christ Jesus." We can boldly step forward in faith, guided by God's peace and the assurance that our decision would not violate His Word. As we honor God with our obedience, He orders our steps.

As God's possession, we are called to love Him and love His people. Ultimately, the call to Thomas and to us is the same: bring glory to God and bring others to Him. The *how* we do that is custom designed by our Creator. Scripture uses calling and vocation interchangeably. Author and television host Paula Faris describes calling this way: "You have two callings: faith and vocation. Your 'faith' calling is your purpose, why you are here on the earth. Your 'vocation' calling is the vehicle, the conduit, by which you will fulfill your purpose."[5]

We accomplish our purpose through our passion and gifts in God-designed ways. Dr. Naomi Dowdy shares, "An anointing comes from your gift, but grace comes upon your life and it is out of God's grace that you will function."[6] God blesses or anoints our unique purpose for His glory. He gives us the grace to walk worthy of our calling, share the gospel, and treat others in a way that honors the name of Christ.

Finally, 1 Peter 2:9 says that God calls us to declare His praises and show others His goodness. We must first believe that God *is* good, loving, merciful, and just before we can express His character to others. Hebrews 11:6 shares this: "And without faith it is impossible to please God, because anyone who comes to him must believe that he exists and that he rewards those who earnestly seek him."

Thomas demonstrated brave faith to trust Jesus, follow Him, and lead others to Him. We must be brave enough not only to believe that God exists but also that He rewards those who seek Him. The Enemy wants us to believe the lies that God is *not* good, that He is *not* trustworthy, and that He *cannot* use us. The Enemy attempts to convince us that we have nothing to offer Jesus and tries to influence us to keep our distance from Him. Jesus invites us to come closer anytime doubt tries to crowd out faith.

As we move from a starting place to a sending place, we need to leave behind anything that keeps us marginalized or ineffective. This includes both internal and external barriers that stem from a place of unbelief. Poet and Bible teacher Jackie Hill Perry shares, "The soil from which all sin grows is unbelief. We counter unbelief through the faith that comes from understanding God's character. As we study the history of His dealings with mankind, His Word reveals Him to be unchangeable and good . . . completely wise . . . holy, and fully trustworthy. Faith in God replaces unbelief."[7]

Unbelief preys on our vulnerabilities in unexpected ways. It threatens our confidence in God when a sick loved one does not recover. It chokes our progress when a dream becomes crushed by divorce. It casts a shadow over our future when we encounter devastating financial loss.

We may struggle to believe that God cares. Brave faith believes that Jesus gave His life for us, rose from the dead, and ascended to heaven where He intercedes for us. We may struggle to believe an answer is on the way. Brave faith believes that God is fully trustworthy in the wait. We may struggle to believe that God will empower us to lead through the challenges of life. Brave faith believes God will impart a greater anointing and sphere of influence to us through the Holy Spirit as we trust in Him.

We may feel unworthy for God to use us to show His goodness to others when we live in the shadow of our past. We remove *internal* barriers of fear and shame through our understanding and acceptance of God's grace. We may experience the opposition of *external* barriers as we seek to move forward in God's call on our lives. These may come in the form of financial pressures, a loss of security, or relational challenges. We remove the barriers to bravery through the encouragement found in Titus 3:4–7:

But when the kindness and love of God our Savior appeared, he saved us, not because of righteous things we had done, but because of his mercy. He saved us through the washing of rebirth and renewal of the Holy Spirit, whom he poured out on us generously through Jesus Christ our Savior, so that, having been justified by his grace, we might become heirs having the hope of eternal life.

We are coheirs with Christ. When we experience the goodness of God, we exercise our calling to serve others. We may not feel fully equipped yet, and that's OK. We just have to give Jesus our yes and take our next steps with Him.

Fear of the unknown can cause us to question if we're brave enough to face what may lie ahead. When Thomas accepted the call to be an apostle, we can be sure he navigated a myriad of emotions. We don't have to have all the answers when God calls us to a new assignment. Jesus won't leave us in a place of uncertainty. As authors, we have both found this to be true in our lives. Hubert shares, "I didn't have all the answers when God stirred me to plant a church in Charlotte, North Carolina, as a young minister. We leaned completely on the goodness of God. He sustained us for six months without a salary and grew our church to four hundred people in five years. We saw miracles and salvations as we stepped out in faith."

Angela adds, "I didn't have all the answers when Dale and I left all our family to answer God's call into ministry. We moved across the United States to join the staff of a church in Fredericksburg, Virginia. I didn't have all the answers when I stared down years of infertility and difficult medical treatments. On the other side of obedience is blessing. We experienced the favor of God as we became the lead pastors throughout thirty years of ministry, and He gave us two beautiful children."

Do you sense God calling you out of one season and into the next? If so, don't wait until you have all the answers. It will require God-sized risks to answer God-sized assignments. He will empower you for what He asks of you. The call of God does not come without a cost. Obedience to God puts a target on our back to the Enemy. Don't be afraid of his attacks but be aware. Expect the unexpected as you put your faith in God. Although Thomas did not know all it would eventually cost him, he still put his full trust in Jesus and accepted His call. As we continue to look at his life, we will see the ways we become awakened to purpose.

Up Close with Angela

In 2003, God spoke to me through a near-death health crisis and shifted the trajectory of my life. I began to feel ill and experience sharp pain I had never known before. I had no appetite and struggled for several months, losing weight and enduring bouts of excruciating pain. After weeks of doctor visits, I was admitted to the hospital. My heart rate had plummeted to forty-one beats per minute, and my blood pressure hovered dangerously low at 76/40. I spent eleven days in the hospital with nothing to eat or drink until the doctors scheduled an extensive MRI.

Lying on my side in the only position my body could tolerate, completely alone, I watched the screen as the barium reached my stomach and stopped. The forty-five-minute GI test took seven hours. I lay on the cold metal table hour after hour—drink, sit up, roll over, stand up, lie down, drink—and I heard the Lord say to me, "Angela, I know you can worship me in the sanctuary. I want to know if you can worship me here." I have led worship hundreds of times, but this hospital room became holy ground. I sang quietly with tears flowing down my face, "Here I am to worship. Here I am to bow down. Here I am to say that you're my God." That moment of surrender ushered in my miracle.

There are no coincidences in God. A hospital doctor read my films and recognized a picture from his recent studies for medical board exams. He had never seen a patient with it in person. They called in more specialists and finally gave me a diagnosis at 7:00 a.m. the next morning—superior mesenteric artery syndrome. SMA syndrome is a rare, life-threatening disorder where the superior mesenteric artery takes too sharp a right turn. The first portion of my intestines, my duodenum, compressed the artery, acting as an obstruction. A severely compressed artery kept my stomach from emptying properly. Two days later, a team of specialists decided to perform a duodenal jejunostomy to bypass the affected portion of my intestines and relieve pressure on the artery. Then they would reconnect the stomach to a lower section of the intestines.

The day of surgery marked my low point. We didn't know if I would make it. I remember asking God, "What else could I need to learn? Why is this happening to me?" God reassured me that this did not take Him by surprise. I survived the surgery, and after one more difficult week in the hospital, I went home. I spent months reeling from trauma, adjusting to a scar that ran the length of my torso, and unable to eat solid food. Even in those dark days, God whispered to me, breathing hope into my withered spirit.

While recuperating, I took out a piece of paper and scribbled these words: "I don't understand how this is in Your plan, but I'll trust You anyhow. I can't possibly see what good is there for me, but I'll trust You anyhow." This song completed my first album and became a new way of living for me—learning to trust God's character completely, even when life is out of focus. We never have to fear the call of God and the voice of God. When we taste His goodness, we can trust His promises.

Up Close with Hubert

At seven years of age, I felt an urgency in my heart to submit myself to Christ and bow to Him publicly. It happened at my home church during a week of revival services. The evangelist, Reverend Hudnell, finished his message one evening and called for anyone who wanted to commit their life to Jesus Christ to come to the front of the sanctuary and kneel at the altar to pray.

I sat between my mother and father, about two-thirds of the way back. Even in my young life, I lived with a question in my mind about being ready to meet the Lord if I should die during my sleep. I felt that it would be a big mistake to stay in my seat in the revival that night. I believed Jesus wanted me to follow Him. I looked at my dad and said, "I want to go." He went with me. I called on Jesus to come into my heart, to save me from sin, and make me ready to go be with Him. In one of the greatest nights in my memory, I was "born again." Life changed in that moment; everything became new for me.

As a sixteen-year-old, I read the story about Jesus praying all night. I came to the place where I wanted to help people know Jesus more than I wanted anything else. I wanted to be able to pray for sick people and see them healed by the power of God. I believed God would give me a greater anointing to be a blessing to people if I could pray all night. I hungered to know God better and have the assurance that He knew my name and knew where I lived. So I got on my knees around 11:00 p.m. one evening in the family room of my parents' house in Vanceboro, North Carolina, and prayed.

When I fell asleep around 2:30 a.m. and awoke a little later, I felt so defeated. I had failed to be able to pray all night. However, God knew my strong desire to hear from Him and to receive direction for my life. I saw a difference in my life after that. Bible passages opened up to me in a new way. God gave me answers about major decisions in life that I needed . . . the right university to attend, the right relationships in my life, and eventually, a wonderful wife to be my faithful companion in life. He has blessed us with three daughters and twelve grandchildren that love us.

Those early experiences paved the way for prayer to become a very important part of my daily pattern of life. Around twenty-five years ago, I started my morning prayer time with the Lord's Prayer, praying each phrase very meaningfully. He makes His presence real to me. It has been a great joy to see His hand at work. I shout the message of assurance to you that God gave to me: He cares about you! He knows your name! He knows your address! He is the greatest!

Come Closer

Takeaway
Outcomes originate in prayer.

1. We strengthen the potency of our prayer life as we train our ear to listen for God's voice.
Consider how you will implement the same valuable prayer keys Jesus taught Thomas. As you do, what is one way you are believing for growth in your prayer life?

2. We remove *internal* barriers of fear and shame through our understanding and acceptance of God's grace. We may experience the opposition of *external* barriers as we seek to move forward in God's call on our lives.
Do you sense any internal or external barriers that are hindering you from stepping out of the crowd and into your calling?

3. The crowd may allow us to stay anonymous and unchallenged. The crowd is noisy and full of distractions. However, as we move closer to Jesus through prayer and relationship, we grow in our identity in Him and in our influence with others. We will then impact our culture *for* Jesus.

What is one way God is leading you from your starting place to a sending place?

CHAPTER 3

Awakened to Purpose

When we last saw Thomas, Jesus called him to leave the crowd and become one of His twelve apostles. With this encounter, Thomas began an up-close and personal observation of the three-year ministry of Jesus. Mark 3:14–15 shares, "He appointed twelve that they might be with him and that he might send them out to preach and to have authority to drive out demons." This framework defined their mission. Before the apostles impacted the world with the gospel, they first spent time with Jesus to understand the power and authority behind His words and actions. As we learn the ways Thomas interacted with Jesus, we discover how to stay tethered to the source, tear down strongholds, and tell others our story.

Tethered to the Source—Presence and Proximity

Thomas didn't simply receive an instruction manual from Jesus. He "appointed twelve that they might be with him." As one of the twelve, Thomas had the privilege of experiencing the presence of Jesus daily. The four gospels contain a great deal of what Jesus said and did. In addition, we can be sure there were many occasions when Jesus stopped and said to the apostles, "Let's talk."

Sometimes, He taught them using parables as He addressed the crowds who gathered by the Sea of Galilee and on mountain tops in the heat of the day. At other times, He engaged His closest followers, the apostles, in conversation over a private meal. Through intimate discussions and public debate, Jesus revealed more about Himself and why He came. As they began to understand His purpose, they became awakened to their own.

In Luke 19:10, Jesus said, "For the Son of Man came to seek and to save the lost." His mission involved a battle with the devil, Satan, who resisted His power to deliver people from slavery to sin. Jesus described it this way in Matthew 12:28–29: "But if it is by the Spirit of God that I drive out demons, then the kingdom of God has come upon you. Or again, how can anyone enter a strong man's house and carry off his possessions unless he first ties up the strong man? Then he can plunder his house." The apostles watched as Jesus set people free from debilitating strongholds that the devil constructed in their lives.

On one occasion, they heard Jesus say to a crowd of followers, "For I have come down from heaven not to do my will but to do the will of him who sent me. For my Father's will is that everyone who looks to the Son and believes in him shall have eternal life, and I will raise them up at the last day." (John 6:38, 40) Thomas heard Jesus disclose that He was the sole source of eternal life for all who believe.

He continued to teach the crowd about the cost required of those who would follow Him. Upon hearing it, many disciples deserted Him. At that critical moment, Jesus turned to the twelve apostles in John 6:67–69 and asked, "'You do not want to leave too, do you?' Jesus asked the Twelve. Simon Peter answered him, 'Lord, to whom shall we go? You have the words of eternal life. We have come to believe and to know that you are the Holy One of God.'" Speaking for the apostles, Peter articulated the hope and identity they found in Jesus. As an integral part of this close-knit group of twelve, Thomas agreed, brave enough to stay when many others turned away. He proved his loyalty and remained closely tethered to Jesus.

Proximity proved invaluable for the apostles. Jesus took them *with* Him before He delegated authority *to* them. Soon, they would walk in this authority. They left everything behind for this season of intense training. Scripture indicates a pause between the apostles' appointment and their first assignment. Thomas traveled with Jesus for many extraordinary events during that time. Let's explore three contained in the Gospel of Luke.

In Luke 7:1–10, Jesus and His apostles entered a village named Capernaum, where Jewish elders approached them. They pleaded earnestly with Him on behalf of a Roman officer who loved the Jewish nation and built their synagogue. Without Jesus's intervention, the officer's household servant would soon die. Despite the tension that existed between the Jews and the Romans, Jesus listened with sensitivity. His mission of love and compassion became obvious as He acted without racial or political bias—quite a lesson for Thomas to learn.

As Jesus approached the officer's house, people met Him with a somber message.

> Lord, don't trouble yourself, for I do not deserve to have you come under my roof. That is why I did not even consider myself worthy to come to you. But say the word, and my servant will be healed. For I myself am a man under authority, with soldiers under me. I tell this one, "Go," and he goes; and that one, "Come," and he comes. I say to my servant, "Do this," and he does it. (Luke 7:7–8)

The officer had the faith to believe all that was needed to eradicate sickness was a word from Jesus. Astonished, Jesus turned to the crowd and said, "'I tell you, I have not found such great faith even in Israel.' Then the men who had been sent returned to the house and found the servant well" (Luke 7:9–10). We can imagine how Thomas's faith grew as the apostles absorbed the impact of this miracle.

Jesus demonstrated not only His power over sickness but also His authority over death. As He entered the town of Nain with His apostles, they encountered the funeral procession of a widow's son. Luke 7:12–18 records,

> As [Jesus] approached the town gate, a dead person was being carried out—the only son of his mother, and she was a widow. And a large crowd from the town was with her. When the Lord saw her, his heart went out to her and he said, "Don't cry." Then he went up and touched the bier they were carrying him on, and the bearers stood still. He said, "Young man, I say to you, get up!" The dead man sat up and began to talk, and Jesus gave him back to his mother. They were all filled with awe and praised God. "A great prophet has appeared among us," they said. "God has come to help his people." This news about Jesus spread throughout Judea and the surrounding country.

The Messiah had come. Thomas found himself not in the presence of a mere prophet or teacher, but with the Son of God who held dominion over death. He recognized unrestrained mercy in the way Jesus responded to a mother's depth of pain. Little did he know how he and the apostles would soon need Jesus to intervene in their own crisis.

Jesus got into a boat with them and began a journey across the Sea of Galilee. In the middle of the voyage, a violent storm arose, and the apostles were gripped with fear. In utter desperation, they cried out to Jesus, asleep in the back of the boat. "'Master, Master, we're going to drown!' He got up and rebuked the wind and the raging waters; the storm subsided, and all was calm. 'Where is your faith?' he asked his disciples. In fear and amazement they asked one another, 'Who is this? He commands even the winds and the water, and they obey him'" (Luke 8:24–25).

Several of the apostles were experienced fishermen, familiar with frequent storms that rose without warning. However, as they exhausted their ability to control the boat, they became paralyzed by fear. Although Jesus stayed right there with them, the Gospel of Mark tells us they questioned whether He cared. When they finally turned to Jesus, they witnessed Jesus exercise His authority over both the external forces of nature and the internal stronghold of fear within them. In the aftermath, Thomas continued to process the way Jesus calmed his feelings of helplessness just as He disarmed the power of the storm.

At times, we may struggle to navigate the perilous waters of life. When doubt or fear threatens to overwhelm us, we can become susceptible to the lie that Jesus is absent, unsympathetic, or unwilling to intervene. Pride, one of the Enemy's greatest weapons, tempts us to believe we can handle situations by ourselves. Disappointment tries to pull us *away* from Jesus when what we need most is time *with* Him. We can't allow the tempests of life to disintegrate our faith. Just like Thomas and the apostles, our desperation must drive us to Jesus. We can come to Him in confidence, knowing that He doesn't rebuke *us* in our time of need; He rebukes the storm.

Jesus is our source of security, peace, and stability in every circumstance. He is with us when we receive the cancer diagnosis. He is with us when we wonder how we will pay our mortgage. He is with us when we long for the return of a prodigal child. Only Jesus can steady our fragile hearts. The more we know Him, the more we rely on Him for wisdom and guidance. He isn't intimidated by what intimidates us. He isn't caught off guard by what takes us off balance. He isn't annoyed by what makes us anxious. He enters into our places of suffering—and that changes everything. He alone is worthy of our full surrender and trust.

So far, we've only scratched the surface of the relationship between Jesus and His apostles. In Thomas, we see the value of staying tethered to the source: purpose flows out of presence. Author and foster child advocate Harmony Klingenmeyer says it this way: "The most important thing for us is to get into personal revival . . . to get into the presence of God and hear what He says about us. Because when we do, He enables us to walk out the will and purposes of God. Start not with the works, but in His presence. Start in His presence and you will find grace to obey."[1]

Before Jesus sends us out, He calls us to Himself. As Thomas experienced Jesus's ministry firsthand, he grew in his understanding of His character. He marveled at the magnitude of Jesus's love and mercy as people came to faith in Him and received miracles of healing and deliverance. In a moment, we will travel with Thomas and the apostles on their first assignment, "to preach and to have authority to drive out demons" (Mark 3:14–15). Through this mission, the apostles served a unique role in the formation of the first-century church. To put this in contemporary language, to fulfill our custom-designed assignments in *this* generation, we must be brave enough to tear down strongholds and tell others our story. As we find our identity in Jesus, we are awakened to our God-given purpose.

Tear Down Strongholds—Power and Promise

Just as Jesus remained physically present with Thomas, the Spirit of God lives in us. He empowers us with the authority to tear down strongholds in our lives and in the lives of others. A stronghold is a false belief that cements into a mindset. It develops when the search for identity and security leads to things other than Jesus, such as world religions, humanistic philosophies, financial status, or achievements.

Strongholds can form when we turn to unhealthy coping mechanisms, especially in times of crisis and uncertainty. These may include pornography, overspending, eating disorders, drug and alcohol abuse, overworking, unethical business practices, and illicit sexual behaviors. Pastor Mike Todd shares, "Coping is an attempt to temporarily feel better about a situation you cannot control. Is it something that's just helping you maintain? The word 'maintain' has the connotation that you are nursing it to death. A coping mechanism may be able to get you down the road a little further, but at some point, it's going to lead you to something that won't work anymore. We have choices to interrupt the plan the Enemy has for us and what our nature takes us back to."[2]

Counterfeit sources entice us to feel numb when Jesus invites us to be known. We are known as we find our identity in Him and the truth of His Word. When we feel weak, He is strong. No matter what we face, we don't have to stay bound by the power of strongholds. It is possible to get untangled from uncertainty and cope with it in godly ways. We will experience victory when we choose to place our security safely in Jesus's hands.

When we ground our worth in the Word instead of the world, we can uproot false beliefs and replace them with biblical truths. Romans 12:2 says, "Do not conform to the pattern of this world, but be transformed by the renewing of your mind." As we study God's word, believe His promises, and walk in obedience to His commands, we renew our minds and experience the power of transformation. This process took place gradually in Thomas, just as it does with us.

We won't experience transformation without warfare. In 2 Corinthians 10:3–5, the apostle Paul conveys the expectation that *all* believers will encounter spiritual warfare against the devil. "For though we live in the world, we do not wage war as the world does. The weapons we fight with are not the weapons of the world. On the contrary, they have divine power to demolish strongholds. We demolish arguments and every pretension that sets itself up against the knowledge of God, and we take captive every thought to make it obedient to Christ."

A pretension asserts the claim that it knows more than God about an issue and how to handle it. We need to identify the thought patterns and mindsets that fight against God. They may come from our own strong will or from a lie of the Enemy. In Matthew chapter 4, Satan tempted Jesus to resist the will of His Heavenly Father. He used scripture to demolish Satan's claims. Following Jesus's example, we will experience spiritual breakthroughs as we speak the truth of God's Word, pray, stand firm in our faith, and walk in obedience.

Ephesians 6:13–18 says,

> Therefore put on the full armor of God, so that when the day of evil comes, you may be able to stand your ground, and after you have done everything, to stand. Stand firm then, with the belt of truth buckled around your waist, with the breastplate of righteousness in place, and with your feet fitted with the readiness that comes from the gospel of peace. In addition to all this, take up the shield of faith, with which you can extinguish all the flaming arrows of the evil one. Take the helmet of salvation and the sword of the Spirit, which is the word of God. And pray in the Spirit on all occasions with all kinds of prayers and requests. With this in mind, be alert and always keep on praying for all the Lord's people.

One of our greatest weapons in warfare is worship. We change the atmosphere as we exalt the name of Jesus. We exercise the authority He has given us when we invite Him to invade our situation. Worship is an act of surrender. When we humble ourselves before God, we receive the power and grace we need to overcome strongholds.

As we stay sensitive and available, He will use us to help others experience freedom, just as He used Thomas. We can pray specifically and intentionally for them and watch for open doors and divine appointments. We will be a source of guidance, comfort, and encouragement as we connect them with God's Word and the freedom He offers.

Tell Others the Story—Preaching and Proclaiming

Thomas's relationship with Jesus led to his first temporary mission. Luke 9:1–2, 6 says, "When Jesus had called the Twelve together, he gave them power and authority to drive out all demons and to cure diseases, and he sent them out to proclaim the kingdom of God and to heal the sick. So they set out and went from village to village, proclaiming the good news and healing people everywhere." Not only did people need the apostles' ministry, but the apostles needed to be built-up in their understanding and confidence to use what Jesus gave them. A novice under Jesus's supervision, Thomas received the preparation for what would later become his life's mission.

We can only imagine what those early moments of ministry must have been like for Thomas. As he took his first step, perhaps he wondered, "Will anyone listen to me share about the kingdom of God? What if nothing happens when I lay hands on someone who is sick?" Although Scripture doesn't share a behind-the-scenes account, Thomas bravely believed what Jesus said and obeyed what He sent him to do.

When the apostles returned, they withdrew with Jesus to a quiet place and shared stories for hours. Thomas could hardly contain his excitement. "Jesus, I prayed for a woman with leprosy and saw her instantaneously healed! I encountered a man held hostage by a demonic spirit and watched God set him free. People believed our message, Jesus. They are so excited to know that You are here. . . ."

Although we can't experience the physical presence of Jesus, He is not distant or indifferent to us. Just as He was with Thomas, He said, "I will be with you" (John 13:33). As we stay in close relationship with Jesus, we are empowered with authority to fulfill our unique God-given assignments in this generation. Without His authority, we will operate solely by human effort. However, we walk *in* authority to the extent that we walk *under* authority. Thomas remained as a part of a tight-knit discipleship group, accountable to Jesus and one another. Kingdom purpose is best developed in community and collaboration, not in silos and isolation.

We can sense how Jesus's authority operates in our lives by the way people are affected by our words and actions. Jesus uses our unique characteristics to accomplish His will and mission for us. It may be the way we communicate with people. It may be our sensitivity to human conditions or our hunger for answers to certain problems. It may be our ability to connect with those with shared experiences. We must be brave enough to believe that God can use any part of *our* story to tell others about *His* story. When we hold nothing back from God, He holds nothing back from us. When we take off the limits, we encounter an unlimited God and become awakened to kingdom purpose.

Author and counselor Bethany Marshall expresses, "The kingdom is His perfect way in our lives. It's His plans and His authority operating and reigning in and through us that are the power and transformation that we need here on this earth. The kingdom gives us hope and expectation of what heaven is going to be like. It's going to be something great and magnificent. Jesus is King. In order to have a King, He needs to have a kingdom. We get to be a part of His Kingdom. Are you a part of it? Do you believe in it? *Kingdom* needs to be a common language because He wants His kingdom here, and He wants His kingdom in us."[3]

Jesus "appointed twelve that they might be with him and that he might send them out to preach and to have authority to drive out demons" (Mark 3:14–15). Thomas and the apostles were not the only ones called to proclaim the kingdom of God. Through Jesus, we can all be brave enough to tell others the story of what He has done in our lives. We cannot be silent. Some will preach from a public platform. Others will pray behind the scenes or quietly invest in hidden places. We reflect the kingdom of God when we love our families well . . . when we advocate for justice . . . when we make the marketplace a mission field . . .

when we serve in the classroom or a political office. No matter what God calls us to do, when we are awakened to His purpose in our lives, we will impact our generation.

Up Close with Angela

Few people exemplify what it looks like to be awakened to purpose more than Hal Donaldson. As the host of the *Make Life Matter* podcast, I had the privilege to interview him and hear his story on episode 79, May 2021.

Hal Donaldson is president of Convoy of Hope, a faith-based, nonprofit organization that leads humanitarian initiatives across the United States and around the world. The author of thirty books, including *Disruptive Compassion*, Hal inspires us to work through a sense of distress or apathy to give others dignity. In our interview, Hal shared moments that changed his life: a haunting word from Mother Theresa, a miracle in one of his lowest seasons, and an encounter that opened heaven over Convoy of Hope.

At twelve years of age, his parents were hit by a drunk driver, instantly killing his father and seriously injuring his mother. He and his siblings were taken in by a young couple, where ten people lived in a trailer for a year.

> Our family experienced the pain, the shame of poverty, but we also experienced the power of kindness. When you are raised poor, you begin a quest not to be poor anymore. I was going to do everything in my power to claw my way out of poverty. I went to college and got two degrees. I began writing books and God opened some doors.
>
> In an interview with Mother Theresa, she stopped and said, "Young man, what are you doing to help the poor?" I told her the truth, that I really wasn't doing much of anything. She said, "Everyone can do something." Those words were haunting.

When I came back to the United States, I loaded up a pickup truck with $300 worth of groceries and handed them out to migrant workers in California. That began the ministry of Convoy of Hope.

Compassion is one thing, but if you want to go beyond compassion, you have to be selfless. God asked me to go to eight major cities and live on the streets for three days and three nights. I walked the streets with a hidden tape recorder interviewing drug addicts, gang members, prostitutes, runaways, and homeless people, and riding with the police on midnight shifts. God used that experience to change me. He broke me and made me a different person. ***God had to do a work in my heart before He could do a work through my hands.*** The heart is the foundation upon which God builds something beautiful. If the heart is flawed, you can only build so high. The more stable the foundation is, the more firm it is.

Through Convoy of Hope, families receive supplies and resources through community outreaches, international feeding programs for nearly 400,000 children a day, job training for mothers, agriculture initiatives, and disaster relief. The organization is on track to feed one million children a day by 2030.[4] Hal Donaldson surely reflects what we have seen in this chapter—our proximity to Jesus determines our purpose.

Up Close with Hubert

Having known Hal for the past forty years, I have seen him consistently reflect the compassionate heart of Jesus. While pastoring a church in northern Louisiana, I coordinated several citywide Convoy of Hope outreach events. As I worked with representatives from Convoy headquarters in Springfield, Missouri, I heard them speak in the most complimentary ways about Hal. He models a life submitted to Christ.

One of the significant aspects of a Convoy of Hope event is the positive interaction across racial lines. I partnered with an African-American pastor as cochairman of the Convoy events that we conducted. He and I brought our volunteers together and supported each other to serve the needs of those who attended. God blessed our efforts as we saw thousands of all ages gather to hear the gospel of Jesus Christ and receive assistance.

Another significant outcome of our Convoy events involved the close connection we developed with city officials. After I visited with the city mayor, he encouraged us to use the city convention facilities and joined me to walk the grounds during the event. One year, an unusual development occurred when it began to snow at the time of the event. Without reservation, the mayor simply told us to move inside the convention center to serve the people.

Hal Donaldson has been faithful to carry the message and the outward expression of God's love to the ends of the earth. His example inspired me to serve people with greater sensitivity and compassion.

How encouraging to know that God assigns to each of us a unique role in His kingdom. The more we spend time with Jesus, the more we are molded into His character and enabled to carry out His purpose for our lives.

Come Closer

Takeaway

As the apostles understood Jesus's purpose, they became awakened to their own.

1. Scripture indicates a pause between the apostles' appointment and their first assignment. Thomas traveled with Jesus for many extraordinary events during this time. We explored three instances in the Gospel of Luke where Jesus demonstrated His authority before He delegated authority to the apostles. Name the three conditions that existed and the result when Jesus exercised His authority.

2. A stronghold is a false belief that cements into a mindset. Strongholds can form when we turn to unhealthy coping mechanisms, especially in times of crisis and uncertainty. **Counterfeit sources entice us to feel numb when Jesus invites us to be known.**

In Matthew chapter 4, Jesus used Scripture to demolish Satan's claims. As you review Ephesians 6:13–18, how do these verses empower you to tear down strongholds?

3. As we stay in close relationship with Jesus, we are empowered with authority to fulfill our unique, God-given assignments in this generation. However, we walk *in* authority to the extent that we walk *under* authority. Kingdom purpose is best developed in community and collaboration, not in silos and isolation.

Consider ways to fulfill your God-given assignments in the context of being accountable to other believers.

ENCOUNTER 2

A Setup

One might wonder at this point if Thomas was a man of few words, considering we have come to chapter 4 and he is yet to speak. During the three years he spent in ministry alongside Jesus, we can be certain he consistently engaged in spirited conversations. However, Scripture records only three marked moments where Thomas spoke, each with noted significance. They reveal much about his character and give us a guide to navigating our uncertainties.

We highlighted several instances in the Gospel of Luke where Thomas experienced the miraculous as He walked with Jesus. We now turn to the Gospel of John where we find Thomas in the middle of rising conflict. As Jesus taught and healed people throughout the region, opposition to His ministry grew. The religious leaders of the day became increasingly jealous of Jesus's influence and incensed at His claims of deity. A quick walk through the beginning of the book of John helps us to understand the course of events that led to the second encounter between Thomas and Jesus.

The Rise of Opposition

In John chapter 2, Jesus visited the temple in Jerusalem. Those in political and hierarchical leadership controlled the activity at the temple. Jesus saw the ways they took their liberty to use the temple to buy and sell for their profit. They became infuriated as He overturned their money-making tables and declared, "Stop turning my Father's house into a market!" (John 2:16).

In John chapter 4, Jesus defied the cultural norms of the day when He chose to travel through the region of Samaria and talk to a woman at a well. Her miraculous testimony brought many in her community to faith in Jesus. The religious leaders became threatened by His growing popularity with the large crowds that followed and believed in Him.

In John chapter 5, Jesus met a man at the pool of Bethesda who had suffered from a debilitating condition for thirty-eight years. He commanded the man to get up, pick up his mat, and walk. The Jewish law prohibited him from carrying his mat on the Sabbath. When the religious leaders confronted Jesus, He replied, "My Father is always at his work to this very day, and I too am working" (John 5:17). Jesus not only broke the Sabbath, but He also called God His Father, making Himself equal to God. They considered this blasphemy and refused to accept His authority over them. If *He* had this type of authority, *they* did not. Scripture shares that Jesus stayed away from the region of Judea and taught in private for a short time because they sought to kill Him.

In John chapter 8, we find Jesus back at the Temple, once again teaching in public. The religious leaders seized the moment to confront and challenge Jesus's assertions: "I am the light of the world. My other witness is the Father who sent me" (John 8:12, 18).The dialogue escalated as Jesus distinguished their father as the devil. With a resounding last word, Jesus announced, "Before Abraham was born, I am!" (John 8:58). Jesus made His identity clear as not just a prophet or a good teacher, but the I AM who called to Moses out of the burning bush . . . the I AM, coequal with God, who existed before the creation of the world. To the religious leaders, this constituted blasphemy. They picked up stones, but He slipped away before they could kill Him. Thomas and the apostles witnessed it all. This backdrop set the scene for one of the most dramatic events to date in the life of Thomas.

In John chapter 11, we find the second encounter between Thomas and Jesus. Amid the contentious climate in Judea, Jesus received an urgent request to return to the region. In this passage of Scripture, we discover a divine setup for God's glory and Thomas's growth. Although Thomas remains silent in the first part of this encounter, much simmers under the surface. When we finally hear him speak for the first time, his courageous words slice through the air, thick with tension and alarm. As we explore his test of loyalty to Jesus, we will learn to trust God's timing and direction and lead with confidence in challenging circumstances.

The Request to Jesus

John 11:1–3 says, "Now a man named Lazarus was sick. He was from Bethany, the village of Mary and her sister Martha. (This Mary, whose brother Lazarus now lay sick, was the same one who poured perfume on the Lord and wiped his feet with her hair.) So the sisters sent word to Jesus, 'Lord, the one you love is sick.'"

Lazarus and his sisters were among Jesus's closest friends and most devout followers. They lived in Bethany within the region of Judea, an area where opposition to Jesus posed an imminent threat. Their home became a haven for Jesus to rest and a hub to teach the principles of the kingdom of God. Away in ministry, Jesus received troubling news; Lazarus had become gravely ill. Although Mary and Martha's words did not contain a direct request, their urgent message implied the expectation that Jesus would come quickly and heal Lazarus.

John 11:4–15 continues,

When he heard this, Jesus said, "This sickness will not end in death. No, it is for God's glory so that God's Son may be glorified through it." Now Jesus loved Martha and her sister and Lazarus. So when he heard that Lazarus was sick, he stayed where he was two more days, and then he said to his disciples, "Let us go back to Judea."

"But Rabbi," they said, "a short while ago the Jews there tried to stone you, and yet you are going back?"

Jesus answered, "Are there not twelve hours of daylight? Anyone who walks in the daytime will not stumble, for they see by this world's light. It is when a person walks at night that they stumble, for they have no light."

After he had said this, he went on to tell them, "Our friend Lazarus has fallen asleep; but I am going there to wake him up."

His disciples replied, "Lord, if he sleeps, he will get better." Jesus had been speaking of his death, but his disciples thought he meant natural sleep.

So then he told them plainly, "Lazarus is dead, and for your sake I am glad I was not there, so that you may believe. But let us go to him."

The news of Lazarus's illness prompted a teaching moment for Thomas and the apostles. Rather than return as requested, Jesus chose to stay until the unthinkable happened. However, His reasons were not what you might expect. We will examine His words and actions step-by-step to see not only what He chose to do, but why He chose to do it.

The Response of Jesus

For God's Glory

Despite their impassioned plea, Jesus delayed for two more days. At first glance, He might seem uncaring or uninterested in Lazarus. Perhaps some thought He refused to come due to the threat level in the area. They would soon realize the intent in His delay. Jesus wanted *only* to show up when His arrival would bring the greatest glory to His Heavenly Father, His premium priority. The experience would also serve to increase the faith of Thomas and the apostles.

He responded, "This sickness will not end in death. No, it is for God's glory so that God's Son may be glorified through it" (John 11:4). He came to earth with the glory of God the Father upon Him. His earthly mission was to bring glory to His Father, and the Father glorified the Son. John 1:1–2 says, "In the beginning was the Word, and the Word was with God, and the Word was God. He was with God in the beginning." The apostle John goes on to explain in verse 14, "The Word became flesh and made his dwelling among us. We have seen his glory, the glory of the one and only Son, who came from the Father, full of grace and truth."

The glory of God can seem like an intimidating or vague concept. Several definitions of *glory* amplify its meaning for us: "high renown or honor won by notable achievements; magnificence or great beauty."[1] Exodus 15:11 exclaims,

> Who among the gods
> is like you, LORD?
> Who is like you—
> majestic in holiness,
> awesome in glory,
> working wonders?

The splendor or bliss of heaven: Psalm 19:1 says, "The heavens declare the glory of God; the skies proclaim the work of his hands."

Praise, worship, and thanksgiving offered to a deity:

> You are worthy, our Lord and God,
> to receive glory and honor and power,
> for you created all things,
> and by your will they were created
> and have their being." (Revelation 4:11)

Thomas and the apostles did not yet understand the way God's glory would be revealed in the extraordinary events that would soon unfold. Spoiler alert: they would witness a never-saw-that-coming miracle in the life of Lazarus. However, their current reality presented this dismal fact: in their delay, Lazarus died.

Although we have the benefit of reading ahead to the end of the story, Thomas experienced moments with Jesus in real time and embraced them with curious thought. Thomas studied the measured way in which Jesus answered His critics. He pondered the artful way in which Jesus posed probing questions. He analyzed the unconventional way in which Jesus chose assignments. With each new experience, Thomas sought clarity as he saw the composite sketch of Jesus drawn before his very eyes. Jesus was everything he had ever wanted and nothing he had ever expected.

For us, the picture of Jesus is complete—the Bible reveals His nature. Yet, like Thomas and the apostles, we can still struggle to truly understand Jesus and His ways. Although the Bible is complete, we can't read the end of our own story. Doubt and disappointment bleed into the margins of our unread pages. Our limited knowledge threatens to obscure our ability to believe that God wants the best for us. The more we study God's Word, however, the more we know and trust the character of the Trinity: our Heavenly Father, Jesus His Son, and the Holy Spirit. David penned a powerful truth that steadies our hearts in uncertain times. Psalm 139:16–18 says,

> Your eyes saw my unformed body;
> > all the days ordained for me were written in
> > your book
> > before one of them came to be.
> How precious to me are your thoughts, God!
> > How vast is the sum of them!
> Were I to count them,
> > they would outnumber the grains of sand.

We are known and loved by our Creator. Our days aren't haphazard. They're orchestrated by design. God's ways, higher than ours, are completely trustworthy. Framed by this truth, we welcome surrender into our lives. One critical question changes the way we view our circumstances. In Jesus's response, we discover ours: "How can God use this for His glory?" This shift in perspective helps us to trust God's timing and direction, especially when we don't understand what He is doing. **Our questions about God's timing are opportunities for God's glory.** When we seek God's glory above all else, we leverage adversity for our spiritual growth. We can place our hope fully in Him. Yet, this can prove difficult when we experience the pain that can come with a delay, most certainly the case for Mary and Martha.

Trust God's Timing

John 11:5–6 says, "Now Jesus loved Martha and her sister and Lazarus. So when he heard that Lazarus was sick, he stayed where he was for two more days." The apostle John described this family's close relationship with Jesus as one hallmarked by love. So why delay?

We cannot imagine the anguish that Mary and Martha felt when Jesus did not show up before Lazarus died. How could He do this to them when they had opened their hearts and their home to Him? They buried their beloved brother without the knowledge that Jesus had a greater plan. They processed their deep disappointment without comprehending the coming victory disguised as a divine delay.

What do we do when we don't understand God's timing? We pray for a baby only to endure a painful season of infertility. We invest everything we have into a business only to see it fail. We fight for our marriage only to experience the heartbreak of divorce. We may doubt God's love when we think He's late. We may begin to question His character when it seems He didn't show up in the way we thought He should. We may become disheartened when a delay causes the death of a dream or our hope.

Or we can be brave enough to believe that while we wait, God works. We don't take a passive posture while waiting. Instead, we actively cooperate with the Holy Spirit when we pray for God's glory to be revealed in and through every situation. Until heaven is our home, we will experience seasons of adversity in this life. We trust God's sovereignty and His goodness whether His answer at the time is yes, no, or not yet.

Tara-Leigh Cobble, creator and host of The Bible Recap podcast, and the founder of D-Group writes, "The Father can be trusted to hear our prayers, sift through them, and answer with whatever is best. Everyone who asks receives! That means there's no such thing as an unanswered prayer—He answers all of them, with yes, no, or wait. We tend to forget that no and wait are answers too. God doesn't always give us what we ask for, because sometimes He has better ideas, but He always hears and responds to us. That's what a good father does. And He's where the joy is!"[2]

When we're worried about an outcome, we can try and control a situation rather than release the timing to God. We may overthink and procrastinate a decision. Or we may resort to manipulation to force the fulfillment of our desires. Philippians 4:6–7 says, "Do not be anxious about anything, but in every situation, by prayer and petition, with thanksgiving, present your requests to God. And the peace of God, which transcends all understanding, will guard your hearts and your minds in Christ Jesus." Peace settles the disquiet of our soul when fear tells us we are facing a hopeless situation.

Peace also helps us to sense God's timing and stay centered in His will. Sometimes God leads us to stay, and other times He leads us to go. We need the wisdom to know the difference. Otherwise, we can run ahead of God or lag behind Him. We may have the right idea from God but not the right timing. The presence of a need does not always mandate immediate action.

When we act impulsively, even with the best of intentions, we can easily make mistakes. Discipline and discernment keep us from rushing headfirst into danger. We have to be brave enough to let God dictate the pace.

We can ask God to help us wait, not just on a desired outcome, but wait on *Him*. The prophet Isaiah wrote in chapter 40:31:

> But those who hope in the LORD
>   will renew their strength,
> They will soar on wings like eagles;
>   they will run and not grow weary,
>   they will walk and not be faint.

When we seek the giver more than the gift, adversity becomes a catalyst for growth. We find the strength and endurance we need when we become desperate for Jesus more than anything else. When we live to know Jesus and make Him known, we experience supernatural contentment and peace in His presence.

Jesus wanted Thomas to know *Him* more than to know what He could do. He taught Thomas the value of divine timing. Lazarus suffered in dire need, yet Jesus did not hurry to him at that exact moment. When it seemed to make the most sense for Jesus to return to Judea, He stayed. Then, when it seemed too late for Lazarus, Jesus wanted to go back. The apostles, clouded by confusion and concern, allowed fear to override their complete trust in Jesus. In a sneak peek of what's to come, Jesus's resolve provoked a tipping point for Thomas and provided a setup for him to speak up. We will soon see him rise above his internal conflict and issue a bold challenge.

Trust God's Direction

In John 11:7 Jesus shared His divine desire with the apostles: "Let us go back to Judea." Jesus's statement of intent stunned them. They met His decision with immediate objection. John

11:8 continues, "'But Rabbi,' they said, 'a short while ago the Jews there tried to stone you, and yet you are going back?'" Conspicuously absent from their reaction was a hearty show of support. In place of a resounding, "Yes, Lord, wherever You want us to go, we will go," stood one tiny word: *"But."*

"But Jesus, the religious leaders want to kill You. We don't know if we can protect You if You go back. We're not even sure we can protect ourselves."

"But Jesus, look at all the ministry opportunities right here where we are. You don't need to put Yourself in harm's way."

"But Jesus, this decision doesn't make any sense. Lazarus is dead. What's the point of going back now?"

"But."

The apostles made valid points: they faced grave danger, and the risks seemed worthless. Their protests likely came from a place of genuine concern for Jesus's well-being. Jesus was not unaware or ill-informed; He *wanted* to go back to Judea.

Because the apostles didn't know or understand the purpose behind His shift in direction, they became the voice of opposition. Before we are too quick to judge their reaction, doubt and uncertainty can cause us to resist God when He says to move. **When we seek self-preservation instead of full surrender, we stifle our spiritual growth and minimize our impact for the kingdom of God.** When God's direction is met with our hesitation, we may find ourselves flooded with questions.

"But God, I don't know what will happen to me if I take this step of faith. I don't think I'm ready for that."

"But God, everything is going well here. I don't want to manage a new learning curve. Don't ask me to start over."

"But God, this doesn't make any sense. I don't see any purpose in it."

We won't always know the *why* when God asks something of us. If we wait until we fully understand God's purpose, we may never operate in obedience. God may lead us to leave when it seems to make more sense for us to stay. At times, God asks us to start something new just when we've grown comfortable with the familiar. When we feel unsure or overwhelmed, our fear does not have to dictate our decisions.

- Our fear can be overcome by our confidence in His presence.
- Our fear can be overcome by our understanding of His love.
- Our fear can be overcome by our reliance on His power.

When we know God is with us, we can trust Him to lead us to an unknown place. He gives us the wisdom to navigate challenges that may come. Anytime He makes His direction clear to us, we are faced with the choice to be brave enough to believe and go with Him no matter what. Regardless of the risks ahead, Jesus insisted on returning to Judea. We will soon see the value of that decision.

The Reveal from Jesus

At this pivotal moment in our second encounter, Thomas heard Jesus make a startling revelation. John 11:11–15 says,

> "Our friend Lazarus has fallen asleep; but I am going there to wake him up." His disciples replied, "Lord, if he sleeps, he will get better." Jesus had been speaking of his death, but his disciples thought he meant natural sleep. So then he told them plainly, "Lazarus is dead, and for your sake I am glad I was not there, so that you may believe. But let us go to him."

Thomas and the apostles reeled from the devastating news. Hope evaporated into thin air as Jesus revealed that Lazarus's condition had deteriorated to the point of death. Yet, these verses contain the not-so-obvious reveal—the condition of the apostles' hearts. With the words, "Let's return to Judea," Jesus made His desire known. Whether a firm suggestion or an implied command, His invitation had fallen on deaf ears. Jesus then disclosed two motivations to entreat the apostles to go back with Him. First, Jesus spoke of Lazarus as "*our* friend," not just "*My* friend." He reminded Thomas and the apostles of their relationship *with* Lazarus and their responsibility *to* Lazarus. Second, Jesus affirmed His determination to go to him with an appointed purpose. Once again, His resolution met their reluctance.

Their protests seemed innocent enough. After all, they didn't know what Jesus knew . . . they couldn't comprehend what lay ahead. Fear kept them from obedience. Apathy pulled them away from their divine assignment. They didn't believe this need justified a decision that would put Jesus, and them, in danger. They disassociated themselves from responsibility to Lazarus and rationalized their disobedience to Jesus. Their solution required the bare minimum of input and accountability: "Just let Lazarus sleep it off." Jesus knew that Lazarus didn't need rest. He needed resurrection. Lazarus needed what only Jesus could do.

Jesus challenged their heart posture and exposed their attitude. They allowed other things to get in the way of someone who needed Jesus. He reminded them—and us— that people matter most. We must trust the compassion of Jesus and develop the faith to believe Him even when we don't understand what He's asking of us. Who are we to decide whether or not someone deserves to meet Jesus? Do we counter Jesus's invitation with our human reasoning? Do we withhold the compassion and grace Jesus wants to demonstrate through us because it's inconvenient or requires risk? What if someone's salvation . . . their deliverance . . . their healing . . . their freedom . . . waits on the other side of our obedience?

We are called to bring Jesus to people. He can use someone else in our stead, but He wants us to be a part of the miracle. We will never regret giving God our *yes*. Share the gospel. Get in community. Give generously. Stay openhanded in service. Love sacrificially. Embrace God's heart for the widow, the orphan, the broken, the confused, and the wounded. Bless those who persecute you for His name. Be brave enough to obey God even in the face of opposition. Welcome every opportunity to live in kingdom purpose and be Jesus to someone.

Jesus sought to heal more than a temporary sickness. He wanted to heal Thomas and the apostles from anything that hindered them from their kingdom purpose. Perhaps Jesus locked eyes with Thomas as He shared the words, "Lazarus is dead, and for your sake I am glad I was not there, so that you may believe. But let us go to him" (John 11:14–15).

His unspoken promise unleashed Thomas's potential. *Now you will see, Thomas, that Lazarus's pain will not be in vain. Mary and Martha's heartbreak will not be wasted. Something is going to happen in your life that would not happen any other way. Your faith will grow beyond what you could imagine.*

Something shifted in Thomas. Up to this point, he had been silent. In a moment, we will read his first recorded words in Scripture. With Jesus's third and final declaration, "Let us go to him," courage rose to the surface in Thomas. The setup was complete.

Up Close with Angela

Life often feels like one big lesson in trust. The circumstances surrounding our choices may change, but the core question remains: Do I truly trust God? Sometimes, He asks us to trust Him and move forward through uncharted territory and unexpected shifts. Other times, He asks us to be still and wait. Perhaps the most difficult trust test for me is to be brave enough to believe He has a greater plan when He says no.

As the founder of Voice of the Voiceless, one of the greatest joys of my life has been my nearly twenty trips to Africa. I worked with kids' camps, women's conferences, and climbed Mount Kilimanjaro for clean-water wells. Over time, God narrowed my focus to empower women in rural regions, especially pastors' wives, through microenterprise programs and education initiatives. While planning my sixth trip to the continent I love, for the first time concerning Africa, I heard a God-sized no in my spirit. Well, honestly, it felt more like a punch to the gut. I delayed and denied it, especially because I intended to bring a full team for a kids' camp in Ghana that had already begun to raise support. I knew what I had to do. The following comes from my journal entries, February 20, 2012: "I'm sitting on a plane on my way to Monrovia, Liberia. Before I ever went to Africa, a dear friend gave me a large poster from a Reinhard Bonnke crusade in Africa. It hung on my unfinished basement wall until, sadly, it became lost during a house renovation. Now, this is a full-circle moment. Let me explain."

I agonized up to the eleventh hour about canceling the trip to Ghana. I discussed my feelings with my husband and resolved to obey God's direction and timing even though I didn't understand. I went to bed intending to let each team member know the next day. I woke up that next morning to tell my team (with zero explanation I could provide other than that God said no) and before I even got out of bed, I clearly heard the name Reinhard Bonnke. I dismissed it but then decided to look up Christ for All Nations (CfaN). I had always admired his ministry but had never been on the website.

As I did, I saw Calendar/Events, then "Impartation Breakfast" in Richmond Virginia, just an hour from my home. With no venue listed, I looked for a phone number and called to offer our church as a location for the event. Over a couple of phone calls, we determined we needed a larger space. The woman I spoke with thanked me and invited me and my husband, Dale, to come to the event as VIPs and meet evangelists Bonnke and Daniel Kolenda. Elated, I would soon discover how much more God had in store. We met with their US director, partnered with the event to provide volunteers, and hosted evangelist Kolenda that weekend to preach at our church.

I ministered in concert at a local church that month, and the pastor, from a very traditional denomination, told me at the end of the service that God had told him He would send me to places I had never heard of. That week, I received a CfaN newsletter and in the list of crusades, my eyes fell on a place called Monrovia. I had never heard of it. My heart began to stir, and I received a confirmation in my spirit through a conversation at ministers' retreat that following week.

I registered to attend the crusade and invited another friend to join me. We prayed and fasted about finances, and the very night we agreed in faith to go, the Lord provided all of our trip completely paid! So now I *knew* God wanted me to go on the trip, but I still had no idea why! I received several prophetic words from people who didn't know each other at all, who saw me ministering in a healing service, standing in front of a large crowd, and undergoing strong demonic attacks but standing strong.

Here is a summation of my personal journal entries throughout this trip. I experienced the power of the Holy Spirit in profound, undeniable ways. It was supernatural, so to try and explain it in the natural isn't possible. During the crusade week, Daniel Kolenda asked me to sing at the crusade in the morning for nearly 50,000 pastors, wives, and leaders. I sang "Break Every Chain" and heard testimonies of witches who came to subvert the crusade and instead surrendered their lives to Jesus Christ. I joined the group of pastors evangelist Bonnke invited to lay hands on all the prayer requests that had been turned in for healing. I witnessed a young girl healed from blindness just mere feet from where I stood, as a liquid substance poured out from her eyes. She could see for the very first time. I had devotions in a small group with my hero of the faith, Reinhard Bonnke, before God called him home. I witnessed hundreds of thousands of people who had walked from far and wide, lining open fields, to encounter God. And as if all these events were not enough, I received healing from the trauma of a situation that had wounded me deeply. I came home whole.

Are you ready for this? The dates of the crusade in Liberia were the EXACT DATES I would have been in Ghana with the kids' camp team. Immediately, I could see why God told me no. It was a setup! He knew what only He could know. He directed as only He could direct.

Our job is not to know why, but to trust the voice of the Holy Spirit and obey. When we trust His timing and direction, even when we don't understand, the outcome is supernatural.

Up Close with Hubert

Sometimes it seems God asks us to take steps in faith without the full understanding of His timing. However, we can move forward with deep-settled peace that reassures us we are in His will. While pastoring a large, thriving church, I realized my work there was finished. We welcomed two hundred new members during the previous year and watched altars filled at the end of services. It appeared that God intended for me to stay put. Not so.

Although painful to leave the beautiful people of that church, we sensed God's clear guidance in our decision. We did not yet know our next steps; however, we obeyed without a tinge of fear. My wife, our three daughters, and I spent a summer with extended family, praying and seeking God's timing. At the end of the summer, we felt led to relocate to Springfield, Missouri, and enroll our daughters in school. Within a few more weeks, two experiences made it clear that we were receiving God's timing for the next step. One day, as we drove through a neighborhood, we saw a friend of our extended family standing on the side of the street. A missionary to Africa, he and his family were soon to return there for a four-year term. After sharing our need to relocate, he made his home available for us to rent, and even included the furniture until ours arrived. We moved into it and enrolled our daughters in the appropriate schools for our neighborhood.

The second confirmation involved a divine appointment with an administrator at Evangel University in Springfield, Missouri.

My wife and I were walking in a store when we recognized and greeted him. We learned that a position at the university would soon be vacant. We thanked him for the information, and I made an appointment to meet with the president of the university. He invited me to apply for the position, and I soon received his invitation to accept it. With confirmation in my heart and in the hearts of my family members that this revealed the hand of God at work, I received this new assignment from the Lord.

I believe we should ask God for His will to be done in our lives, pray to Him in the name of Jesus, study His Word, and watch how He gives us His will. I believe He gives it to us, even when we don't know He is doing it. Sometimes, it is not until a later time that we realize God's faithfulness led us into positions that expanded our opportunities to serve more effectively. We simply have to trust Him.

During the fifteen years that followed, my ministry as one of the vice presidents of Evangel University included speaking in over five hundred churches and helping to raise $12 million to expand the facilities at the university. In addition, our daughters received their college degrees tuition free.

I am amazed at how God works. With joy, I praise Him for His faithfulness, His love, and His peace. I boldly proclaim that you can trust God's timing.

Come Closer

Takeaway
Our questions about God's timing are opportunities for God's glory.

1. Our limited knowledge threatens to obscure our ability to believe that God wants the best for us. One critical question changes the way we view our circumstances: How can God use this for His glory?
Is there a situation in your life that needs to be reframed with this question?

2. What do we do when we don't understand God's timing? Philippians 4:6–7 says, "Do not be anxious about anything, but in everything, by prayer and petition, with thanksgiving, present your requests to God. And the peace of God, which transcends all understanding, will guard your hearts and your minds in Christ Jesus."
Do you tend to lag behind or rush ahead of God's timing? How do these verses help you experience the peace that while you are waiting, God is working?

3. When God's direction is met with our hesitation, we may find ourselves flooded with questions. We won't always know the *why* when God asks something of us. If we wait until we fully understand God's purpose, we may never operate in obedience.

What parts of "Up Close with Angela" and "Up Close with Hubert" inspire you to take God-sized risks and follow God's direction?

CHAPTER 5

A Step-Up

Jesus made His intent known: He would go to Bethany with or without the apostles. The thought of returning with Jesus provoked intense fear in their hearts. If the enemies of Jesus could kill Him there, the apostles believed they would surely be the next to die. Thomas leveraged an unexpected setup to take an unanticipated step-up. As we watch him lead, we discover several defining characteristics of devoted courage.

John 11:16 says, "Then Thomas (also known as Didymus) said to the rest of the disciples, 'Let us also go, that we may die with him.'" In his first recorded words, Thomas bravely spoke up to align with the purposes of Jesus. He countered the rallying cry of opposition to become the voice of agreement. Thomas could have simply told Jesus, "I want to go back with you, come what may." Instead, he turned to the apostles and declared, "Let us also go." In the face of challenging circumstances, his uncommon courage silenced and steered the others.

The apostle Peter is often recognized as the outspoken, front-and-center leader of the group. However, Thomas demonstrated similar traits of boldness and tenacity to speak up when others would not. The more we observe Thomas, the more we see him in a new light: a brave apostle willing to die for Jesus.

In *All the Apostles of the Bible*, Herbert Lockyer writes this about Thomas:

His attitude at this juncture in Christ's ministry was a sign of his attachment and devotion to Him and marks him as having a love both deep and strong as that of any other disciple. His was a love that counted no sacrifice too great, and, as one of the bravest of the brave, he was willing to go into the very jaws of death in the company of his Lord. Let us, therefore, cease maligning Thomas, accusing him of morbid fear, gloominess, and pessimism. He was a choice spirit, with a nobility and worth of character some theologians have not fairly recognized. His chief characteristic was that of a deep and devoted love ever ready to leave all for Christ, dare all for Christ, and die with Christ.[1]

We cannot allow fear or lack of devotion to keep us from speaking up when needed. Some situations call for silence while others call for our voice. How can we discern the difference? It requires more than knowledge—it calls for wisdom. Knowledge gives us facts, but wisdom interprets those facts accurately and takes appropriate action. James 1:5 says," If any of you lacks wisdom, you should ask God, who gives generously to all without finding fault, and it will be given you." Courageous choices must be bathed in wisdom. Thomas proved himself ready to lead the charge and risk everything for Jesus. His actions were framed by desire, decision, and determination.

Desire

Thomas did not speak up when Jesus initially expressed His intent to return to Judea. However, he quickly reached a point of complete commitment regardless of the outcome. It became imperative to him that he stay closely connected to Jesus. More than anything, Thomas desired what Jesus wanted. His obedience honored Jesus. Pastor Jon Tyson writes this in *Beautiful Resistance*, "Honor is the call to recognize the value in God and one another and to order our relationships around it. Honor is the operating system of the kingdom of God."[2]

Desire is a reflection of whom and what we choose to honor. Like Thomas, our desire to know and follow Jesus must be greater than any other desire. Desires are formed through our will and triggered by our emotional responses. Scripture warns about the dangers of unchecked desires that can lead us into sin. James 1:14–15 says, "Each person is tempted when they are dragged away by their own evil desire and enticed. Then, after desire has conceived, it gives birth to sin; and sin, when it is full-grown, gives birth to death." It is our responsibility to assess our desires to determine whether or not they are informed by the will of God and congruent with the Word of God.

Through God's promises and presence, we renew our minds and place our desires under the lordship of Jesus Christ. The apostle Peter shares this encouragement in 2 Peter 1:3–4: "His divine power has given us everything we need for a godly life through our knowledge of him who called us by his own glory and goodness. Through these he has given us his very great and precious promises, so that through them you may participate in the divine nature, having escaped the corruption in the world caused by evil desires."

Although we can default to the desires of our flesh, we are not powerless against them. This is confirmed in the scientific research of renowned cognitive neuroscientist, Dr. Caroline Leaf. In her book *Switch on Your Brain,* she writes, "Our brain does not control us; we control our brain through our thinking and choosing. . . . We are not victims of our biology. We are co-creators of our destiny alongside God. God leads, but we have to choose to let God lead. We have been designed to create thoughts, and from these we live out our lives."[3]

Godly desires are the starting point to a life of tenacious faith. When we love and honor the Lord more than anything, we submit our desires to His. John 15:7 says, "If you remain in me and my words remain in you, ask whatever you wish, and it will be done for you." Once we know our thoughts are consistent with His thoughts, we gain the confidence to move from desire to decision.

Decision

Thomas stood at a crossroads. He could not escape the gravity of the moment. Gripped by the realization that he could suddenly be without Jesus, Thomas became desperate to make a decision: "Do I stay or do I go?" Thomas weighed the options, assessed the risk, and decided the reward would be worth the cost. His answer would shape his destiny: "Jesus is going back, and He's not going without me."

Thomas didn't say, "Let's go watch Jesus raise Lazarus from the dead." Jesus had allowed Lazarus to die, and it appears the apostles did not entertain the possibility of his resurrection. They knew Jesus had the power to do it, as they had witnessed with a widow's son. Jesus knew that the miracle waiting for them in Bethany would build greater faith in Thomas. In John 11:14–15 Jesus said, "Lazarus is dead, and for your sake I am glad I was not there, so that you may believe." Thomas chose to follow Jesus out of obedience, not from a place of full understanding of the future. His decision unlocked new levels of faith.

Raised a Hebrew, scholars concur that Thomas would have most certainly been influenced by the devoted courage of three brave Hebrew young men whose story is found in Daniel chapter 3. Shadrach, Meshach, and Abednego knew they could be killed if they refused to bow down to worship an image of gold built by the King of Babylon. They boldly took a stand in verses 16–18, "King Nebuchadnezzar . . . if we are thrown into the blazing furnace, the God we serve is able to deliver us from it, and he will deliver us from Your Majesty's hand. But even if he does not, we want you to know, Your Majesty, that we will not serve your gods or worship the image of gold you have set up." Thrown into a furnace heated seven times hotter than normal, they escaped without even the smell of smoke. **God met their decision with His deliverance**. The king not only released them, but he also honored them and their God. In their actions and those of Thomas, we find a three-step process to follow when we face a significant decision: stop, look, and listen.

- **Stop.** A decision made on the run may prove faulty. The three Hebrew men stood still and remembered their commitment to only offer worship to the one true God of Israel. When the apostles rushed to judgment and resisted Jesus's request, Thomas paused to reconsider his response. We make wise decisions when we wait on God for the open door and the confirmation of His timing.
- **Look.** The facts of a situation can paint a dismal picture unless we view them through the lens of faith. Jan Aldridge, miraculously healed of a rare birth defect at seventeen years of age, writes, "Faith puts a comma where the facts put an exclamation point."[4] Our heroes saw the potential consequences of their choices and placed their full trust in God. Because they were brave enough to believe Him no matter what, their decision made room for the miraculous.
- **Listen.** Amid a contentious culture, we need to learn to listen to the still, small voice of God. Just like Thomas and the three men, we can choose to lead with our convictions rather than our emotions. Even if we hand Him our *yes* with trembling hands, He honors our surrender. Decisions made from a posture of obedience position us for blessing.

God invites us to view our circumstances through a heavenly perspective; He holds the future we cannot see. We get untangled from uncertainty and experience true victory when we rest in the assurance of God's unchanging character. Release the outcome of every decision to Him and trust Him for the strength to stay steady. Once we've made a decision, determination is the grit we need to follow through.

Determination

Thomas refused to allow anything to hold him back from following Jesus, even if it meant death. His determination as a godly leader influenced others to step out as well. When times of uncertainty call for us to lead with confidence, his example provides valuable insight. Godly leaders recognize the ways fear can short-circuit a God assignment. They welcome discomfort rather than maintain the status quo. They often take greater risks than those around them and choose obedience over complacency. Godly leaders cast vision and inspire others to reach their kingdom potential. However, our determination to obey Jesus cannot be contingent upon whether or not others take the journey with us. We are not responsible for the choices others make, but we *are* required to steward well what God entrusts to us.

Gracia Burnham and her husband, Martin, served with New Tribes Mission in the Philippines for seventeen years. On May 27, 2001, rebels from the Abu Sayyaf terrorist group seized the Burnhams and several other guests at a resort and took them as hostages to Basilan Island. In the ensuing 376 days of captivity, they endured unimaginable hardship and emotional fatigue. On June 7, 2002, a firefight between the Philippine military and the Abu Sayyaf group killed Martin. Gracia sustained a serious wound to her leg but gained freedom from her captors.

As the author of *In the Presence of My Enemies*, Gracia said this about Martin's last day in an interview with Angela:

> We knew the military was following us; we could hear them in the distance. We hadn't eaten in 10 days, only salt and water. We were weak and exhausted and thought we were safe because the military never fought in the rain. We set up our hammocks and plastic sheeting and Martin said to me, "Gracia, this doesn't feel like serving the Lord. We've been walking through this jungle for over a year. But let's by faith accept that that's what we're doing. We're serving the Lord

here, and let's do it with gladness." Minutes later, the military came over the hill, opened fire on our captors, and Martin was killed in the crossfire. It was his last words . . . his challenge. That is my new life's theme: I try to figure out what it is God has for me to do and do it with joy.[5]

There is something more dangerous than risking death to follow Jesus; it is the slow death we endure when we approach uncertainty with complacency. Recognize the traps that steal purpose. Apathy causes us to withdraw from the arena of meaningful kingdom contribution. Diluted obedience keeps us from greater effectiveness. We can trade the pitfalls of a passive position for the power and authority we receive in God's presence. Unwavering determination outlasts adversity.

Thomas had faith to believe Jesus in that moment even though he didn't fully grasp the mission. He would soon experience more than he could imagine. Let's continue our story in John chapter 11.

Unmet Expectations

As Thomas approached Bethany with Jesus and the others, he may have wrestled with a myriad of emotions. Had the religious leaders planned an attack? What words could he possibly find to comfort his grief-stricken friends? As they arrived, he became gripped with a dire realization: Lazarus had been in the tomb for four days. The apostles had seen Jesus raise the widow's son and Jairus's daughter within hours of their death. *But four days?* Jewish tradition taught that the soul hovered around the body for three days after which the body, brain, and organs decayed beyond all earthly hope. Lazarus and the impending miracle were out of sight but not out of reach for Jesus.

For Mary and Martha, the wait had been excruciating. People came and went to bring condolences, but Jesus remained conspicuously absent. By the time He arrived, Lazarus lay dead in a tomb. As soon as Martha got word of Jesus's arrival, she left to meet the group at the edge of town. One look at her told Thomas everything. Heartbroken, her first words were heavy with the weight of the emotional toll the experience had taken on her. "Lord . . . if you had been here, my brother would not have died. But I know that even now God will give you whatever you ask" (John 11:21–22).

Martha knew Jesus could have kept this from happening. She not only buried her brother, but she also buried her unmet expectations. Jesus did not allow her palpable pain and unbridled honesty to jar Him. In John 11:23–27 He said,

> "Your brother will rise again."
>
> Martha answered, "I know he will rise again in the resurrection at the last day."
>
> Jesus said to her, "I am the resurrection and the life. The one who believes in me will live, even though they die; and whoever lives by believing in me will never die. Do you believe this?"
>
> "Yes, Lord," she replied, "I believe that you are the Messiah, the Son of God, who is to come into the world."

Thomas absorbed the magnitude of their conversation. He watched as the unwelcome crisis catapulted Martha to deeper levels of faith. Right in the middle of her grief, Martha made a bold confession that Jesus is the Messiah. Although she didn't understand exactly what He planned to do, she knew Him— and that was enough.

Bitterness grows easily in the soil of unmet expectations— but not for Martha. She refused to let anything obscure her devotion. She leveraged adversity into an opportunity for spiritual growth. She allowed the tomb of disappointment to become the tool that leveled up her faith.

Mary remained behind, undeniably exhausted from the steady stream of visitors and heartsick from the loss of her brother. Perhaps she had not yet found the words to say to

Jesus. Each sister processed their pain in unique ways. Whether desperation drives us to confront Jesus or withdraw from Him, His response is the same: He invites us to come closer when pain pulls us away. Martha's words to Mary hold the healing balm for every broken heart: "The Teacher is here . . . and is asking for you" (John 11:28).

Jesus didn't return only to call Lazarus from a tomb. He also came to rescue Mary and Martha from the death grip of confusion and isolation. Face-to-face with Jesus, neither sister held back. Mary threw herself at Jesus's feet, weeping as she poured out the same lament: "If you had been here, my brother would not have died" (John 11:21). Even the Jews who mourned with Mary and Martha wondered aloud why Jesus, the man who opened the eyes of the blind, had not kept Lazarus from dying. Their unmet expectations led to unanswered questions.

We are not immune from confusion when expectations go unmet. We don't have to become stuck in the quagmire of *why*. Instead, we can ask God what He wants to do in and through us and our circumstances. We can bring Jesus our hard questions, but we cannot allow them to create suspicion about His character and cause distance in our relationship. There is no tomb so dark that Jesus cannot reach us.

Jennifer Rothschild author of *Lessons I Learned in the Dark* said this about living with the condition of blindness: "When we are disappointed in life, we can choose to serve our disappointment, or we can serve Jesus *in* our disappointment."[6] We serve our disappointment when we dwell on what we cannot change. That can lead us to blame God for what we thought He should have kept us from or what we thought He withheld from us. We serve Jesus *in* our disappointment when we are brave enough to believe He is worthy of our full surrender no matter what.

Mary and Martha hoped Jesus would do something for them, but He wanted to do something *in* them first. As Jesus talked with the sisters, He didn't defend His delay. He didn't withhold

His emotions either. His two-word response constitutes the shortest verse in Scripture: "Jesus wept" (John 11:35).

His deep empathy for Mary and Martha certainly impacted Thomas. He witnessed an up-close and personal expression of the way Jesus still relates to us today.

The writer of Hebrews says this in chapter 4:15–16: "For we do not have a high priest who is unable to empathize with our weaknesses, but we have one who has been tempted in every way, just as we are—yet he did not sin. Let us then approach God's throne of grace with confidence, so that we may receive mercy and find grace to help us in our time of need."

Jesus is not indifferent to our pain and suffering. Like Mary and Martha, we can come to Him in times of disappointment with raw vulnerability, open hearts, and offer Him our full confession of faith. When we unclench our fists and release our unmet expectations, we find rest in the unending compassion of God.

The Miracle

Jesus arrived at Lazarus's tomb with Thomas and the others to find a large stone covering the entrance. When Jesus ordered the stone removed, Martha countered His request with concerns about the deterioration of her beloved brother. Her hope had died. She couldn't see beyond the limitations of the natural to grasp the spiritual dynamics at work.

However, the miracle lay just beyond the stone. Jesus turned to her and said, "Did I not tell you that if you believe, you will see the glory of God?" (John 11:40)

Sometimes we struggle to let Jesus into the places we've sealed off from Him, believing it is too difficult for Him or too painful for us. We can trust that Jesus moves a stone to heal us, not to wound us. Lisa Whittle shares this in *The Hard Good*:

When we don't deal with our brokenheartedness, it leads to more woundedness. . . .

If we're to have any chance of opening our hearts back up, again, we will first have to tend to the places we've been wounded. We'll need to be honest about them, call them exactly what they are, and let God do the soul surgery required for us to move forward. . . .

We don't happen into hopelessness—we neglect ourselves there. Opening our hearts back up has nothing to do with other people. It has everything to do with how much we believe God. If we believe He has us, loves us, and can be trusted, we can live without the fear that holds us back.[7]

When we stare at the stone of what seems impossible, we may hesitate to believe that Jesus can change our situation. It may appear that our marriage, our finances, or our health have deteriorated beyond all hope. In tender moments like these, we receive two different invitations that challenge us to accept, in faith, the word of God. They might *sound* similar, but they could not be further apart. We need to recognize both the substance and the source.

In Genesis 3:1 Satan asked Eve, "Did God really say?"

In John 11:40 Jesus asked Martha, "Did I not tell you if you believe, you will see the glory of God?"

The first question invites us to doubt the goodness of God and place His character on trial. The other invites us to trust the goodness of God and know His character will sustain us *through* any trial. When we reject the false source, laced with lies, and fully commit to the truth, God can remove any stone that blocks His will. He redeems, restores, and repurposes anything for His glory.

Mary and Martha held their breath as those nearby removed the stone. John 11:43–44 says, "Jesus called in a loud voice, 'Lazarus, come out!' The dead man came out, his hands and feet wrapped with strips of linen, and a cloth around his face."

The atmosphere became electric. The crowd erupted in praise as they witnessed the glory of God on display. Their friend . . . their brother, came out of the tomb—alive. Mary and Martha wept with joy! They had allowed Jesus into their deepest place of private pain and now welcomed their reward. Thomas stood amazed. He had allowed Jesus to call him out of a crowd and into a relationship with Him. He never dreamt what he would see and experience. His determination to follow Jesus at all costs brought him to this moment he would never forget.

Jesus turned toward them and said, "Take off the grave clothes and let him go" (John 11:44). Perhaps Thomas reached up to unwrap the strips of linen and be the first to look into Lazarus's face. A new day dawned . . . all that entangled Lazarus disappeared. At times, grave clothes of uncertainty wrap around our devotion and courage. Cords of our past try to choke out the promise of our future. It takes an encounter with Jesus to be truly free and whole. He calls us to come out of anything that entangles us and come closer to Him. We weren't created to wear grave clothes; we were created to wear garments of grace.

For Thomas, everything had led to this. If he hadn't spoken up to go with Jesus to Bethany, Jesus would have gone without him. But because Thomas had been brave enough to believe, the other apostles also witnessed this miracle for themselves. All along, Jesus had told them this sickness would not end in death. He proved He is the God of the impossible. He knew the end from the beginning for Lazarus, and He knows it for us.

Adversity

Applause doesn't always follow a miracle. Many Jews believed in Jesus as a result of Lazarus's resurrection. When the religious leaders received word, they called an emergency meeting and plotted to kill Jesus. As a result John 11:54 says, "Therefore Jesus no longer moved about publicly among the people of

Judea. Instead, he withdrew to a region near the wilderness, to a village called Ephraim, where he stayed with his disciples."

Few things cause more discouragement than when a victory is followed by a wilderness experience. What did they find in a wilderness? No longer surrounded by adoring crowds, they experienced the lonely arena of desolation. No longer consumed with handling kingdom activity, they held nothing but time. Perhaps they wondered what happened to the enlarged territory they hoped for . . . the new levels of ministry . . . the reprieve from adversity. What started as a setup now looked like a setback. This sudden turn of events may have caught Thomas and the apostles off guard but certainly not Jesus. He knew that the fruit of the miracle would further infuriate the religious leaders, forcing Him and His closest followers to a barren place. For Lazarus to live, something else had to die: Jesus no longer moved freely about the region. However, this short, wilderness season provided the space for conversations that sustained Thomas and the others for the long haul. Things happened there that would not have happened any other way.

Obedience will always bring blessing, but it may not look like we thought it would. If we anticipate resistance, we won't become derailed by doubt or disappointment. Even Jesus, our ultimate leader, faced jealousy and rejection. We may be directly in the center of God's will and still experience opposition.

Satan is relentless in his efforts to kill what God has raised to life in us. Be brave enough to believe that God works even in the wilderness to accomplish His purposes in our lives. Perhaps what looks like a wasteland isn't a waste at all but a space for quiet conversation and deeper relationship with Christ. And that is a setup to step-up.

Up Close with Angela

From January 3–13, 2011, I embarked on an unforgettable adventure to climb Mount Kilimanjaro for water wells. I joined WorldServe International and a team of forty-four climbers to scale Africa's tallest mountain, at 19,340 feet. Throughout my four previous trips to Africa at the time, I had witnessed the devastation brought on by the lack of clean water: more than six thousand people die every day. I bathed the decision to embrace this God assignment in much prayer and conversation. The personal sacrifice involved not only raised funds but raised awareness in profound ways. The high-risk, high-reward aspects of the endeavor also elevated my fears.

What motivates a godly leader to challenge their limitations to accept God assignments? As we study the actions of Thomas in this passage, we identify several criteria.

In his obedience, Thomas chose risk over comfort. God calls kingdom-minded leaders to leave behind complacency in order to inspire others. Few things welcomed discomfort into my life more than climbing Mount Kilimanjaro.

After months of intense preparation and physical training, the day finally arrived! We began adjusting to the altitude while visiting Loibersoit, a remote Maasai village where WorldServe International placed a well. Seeing the villagers' beautiful faces and the difference water made in their lives provided additional motivation for the monstrous task ahead of us.

We began the six-day climb up Mount Kilimanjaro on the Machame Route, the most scenic, but also the most difficult of the open routes. By day, we traversed through four of its ecosystems: rainforest, moorland, alpine desert, and glacial valleys. By night, we hunkered down in small, two-person tents and endured freezing temperatures. We averaged twenty-five thousand steps a day over sixty miles. Our crew of 164, including guides and porters, prepared extraordinary meals, carried large packs, and walked up to five extra miles each day to get fresh water for us to fill our camelbacks.

Everyone who climbs Mount Kilimanjaro sets their hope on one thing: reaching the summit of Uhuru Peak. Despite my determination, during the fourth full day of climbing, that long-coveted desire began to slip away. Our eleven-hour day included the Barranco Wall, an ominous but rewarding challenge. By the late afternoon, severely nauseated and unable to keep water down, I began to have trouble focusing. I slowed my pace to hike through the Karanga Valley in solitude. With just enough phone battery to listen to worship music, God ministered to my weary soul and—literally—led me through the valley. As I looked up at what still lay ahead for me to climb, I thought to myself, "I'm so done. There's no way I can get up this."

I leaned forward and put my head on my poles to rest. I emptied my backpack of water, trying to lighten my load. Sinking to my lowest point, I struggled to get a deep breath. Just then, Sam, one of our guides, stepped in front of me and gently whispered, "Just follow my pace. Follow my steps."

I put one foot in front of the other until he led me to base camp of the summit at sixteen thousand feet. Doctors deemed my heart rate too elevated and breathing too shallow to continue. I cried and soaked in the presence of God as I experienced my own personal summit at sundown on the edge of the cliff at Barafu Camp.

At 1:00 a.m. as many on the team made their attempts to summit, several of us walked through the darkness back down the mountain. When we stopped once to turn off our headlamps and take in the spectacular stars, we turned around to watch the line of small lights, our team members, make their way to the summit. Deep disappointment began to grip the tender places of my heart. But God not only speaks on the mountaintop moments in our lives; He also speaks in the valley and in the darkest of nights.

I have carried the moment Sam moved in front of me, not only down the mountain, but through life. We are called, not to an outcome, but to obedience. We are asked to follow God's footsteps and listen intently to His voice, especially in difficult times. Through this experience, God gave me this vivid spiritual analogy of His encouragement found in Galatians 5:25: "Since we live by the Spirit, let us keep in step with the Spirit." Follow the Spirit . . . and let Him lead.

Whether or not you ever climb Mount Kilimanjaro, you will scale spiritual mountains in life. Step into your calling. Fear will always list the reasons you can't. Faith finds a way. Welcome discomfort. Embrace the risk. Accept the God-sized assignments that stretch you beyond your ability. If you look at your life and feel you can do everything in your own strength, perhaps you are not dreaming big enough dreams for God. God uses ordinary people to do extraordinary things. He is the extra. All He requires of us is obedience.

Up Close with Hubert

Is it worth it to take risks to accomplish God's will for your life? I offer a resounding yes. My wife and I took our greatest risk in ministry when, at the age of twenty-seven, we decided to move to Charlotte, North Carolina, to start a new church. With my wife Glenda, six months pregnant, and two-year-old Angela in tow, we headed toward Charlotte in a car with 120,000 miles on it. We did not even have equity accumulated in a home. The challenges were real.

Originally, the North Carolina Assemblies of God district officers planned to appoint Reverend Conant, a pastor from Pennsylvania to lead the church. Rev. Conant would coordinate seventy-five to one hundred volunteers from churches in the southeastern United States who would give five days and nights in Charlotte to go door to door and invite people to the first services. With his son driving, Rev. Conant started the trip from Pennsylvania to Charlotte for a strategic planning meeting for the new church. When his son fell asleep at the wheel, their car left the highway and crashed. Rev. Conant died in the accident.

I had been serving for two years as the North Carolina Assemblies of God state youth director. One evening on one of our trips through Charlotte, my eyes fell upon the lights of the city, and my heart and mind became gripped with the desire to see God transform people there. I knew there would be many who found themselves in desperate need of the Savior, the Lord Jesus Christ. Shocked and deeply saddened at the news of Rev. Conant's untimely death, my spirit again became stirred concerning what would happen to people in Charlotte who needed the Savior.

I made my way down a hallway at the Assemblies of God headquarters building in Dunn, North Carolina, and asked to meet with the state superintendent and the state home missions director. As we talked, I began to share with them how I sensed an urgency for ministry to people in Charlotte. I told them my wife and I would pray about moving to Charlotte to begin the new church if we were approved to go there. They said they would give consideration and prayer to my appointment as the new pastor. When I arrived home that evening, I told my wife that the district officials were considering someone who would become the pastor of the new church in Charlotte. She said, "I think I know who it is." With her added confirmation, we knelt by the sofa that night and committed ourselves to the will of God, whatever it might be. Within a few days, we received the news that we were appointed to go to Charlotte.

God blessed our obedience in miraculous ways. The Assemblies of God handled the purchase of a little over one acre of land on Scaleybark Road for approximately $9,600. They also had two men who were willing to spend time constructing a three thousand square-foot, brick building, which contained a sanctuary, classrooms, offices, and bathrooms. The agreed-upon financial arrangements for the new pastor were for all the bills to be paid first (mortgage payments, utilities, church supplies, and so on) and for the pastor to receive 75 percent of the amount left over. My first month's personal income totaled $265.

With our small house to rent and no payments on our automobile, my wife and I determined that I would concentrate full-time as pastor and put our trust in God for our survival. **We would trust God for our income and trust Him with the outcome.** He placed His blessing upon the work. After starting with twelve people in attendance, within six months there were forty to fifty attending. The offerings increased gradually, and within six months, our income had become $1,000 per month. I loved serving people: visiting the sick, making visits to people in the neighborhood, starting a daily, five-minute radio program called *The Pastor's Phone Call*, and preparing for the ministry of God's Word.

Most of the twelve people who started the church with us came from First Assembly of God Church in Charlotte where Reverend Fortenberry served as pastor. He decided to announce that we were beginning the new church and invited any of his people to help us who wished to do so. He took a risk that could have weakened his own church to help the new church. What he did made a great difference in our progress at Trinity Assembly. God did something miraculous in his church after that. Prior to our beginning the new church, First Assembly's church attendance had consistently been one hundred to one hundred fifty people for many years. After his kindness and generosity to promote the new church, his church attendance grew to three hundred people within the next year.

We were also blessed by other pastors inviting us to share our ministry in their Wednesday night services where they encouraged their people to bring groceries to give to us. We placed our mid-week services on Thursday nights which allowed us to make visits to other churches on Wednesday nights. It meant so much to us to receive the expressions of love from other churches.

With no guarantee of personal income, the risk turned out to be worth it all. People responded to the invitation to believe in Jesus, repent of sin, and be baptized in water. Within the five years we pastored in Charlotte, the church grew to 450 people with a new sanctuary built to accommodate the crowds. Two young men gave their lives to God for full-time ministry and have served faithfully for many years as pastors.

Opportunities arose to produce two record albums and a movie titled *The King Is Coming*. The pastor of the oldest Presbyterian church in Charlotte, Horace Hilton, asked me to lead worship at a weekly, Friday morning, men's prayer breakfast with three hundred men attending from throughout Charlotte. When he planned to take thirty people for a tour of Israel, he invited me to be his guest and sing "The King Is Coming" on the Mount of Olives near Jerusalem. The leader of the Full Gospel Business Men's Charlotte chapter heard about it, and he and his wife paid for my wife to go with us.

Don't hesitate to take risks for God's will in your life when you see confidently that He is arranging things and confirming things for you. He will always bless your obedience.

Come Closer

Takeaway

There is something more dangerous than risking death to follow Jesus; it is the slow death we endure when we approach uncertainty with complacency.

1. In his first recorded words, "Let us also go that we may die with Him," Thomas bravely spoke up to align with the purposes of Jesus.
In what way did this chapter expand your understanding of Thomas and inspire you to step up in the face of challenging circumstances?

2. Thomas weighed the options, assessed the risk, and decided the reward would be worth the cost. His answer would shape his destiny: "Jesus is going back and He's not going without me."
What three-step process can you use when facing a significant decision?

3. Both Mary and Martha met Jesus with the same lament: "If you had been here my brother would not have died." Jennifer Rothschild encourages us, "When we are disappointed in life, we can choose to serve our disappointment, or we can serve Jesus *in* our disappointment."

Mary and Martha hoped Jesus would do something *for* them, but He wanted to do something *in* them first. He drew Martha into a place of confession and Mary out of a place of isolation. What do you sense God is doing *in* you even in the face of unmet expectations?

ENCOUNTER 3

CHAPTER 6

The Place

"*Mah nishtanah halyla hazeh mikol halaylot?* Mama, why do we celebrate Passover? What does this all mean? Why only matzah? Why the bitter herbs?"[1]

"Always the questions, hmm, Thomas?" His mother had come to expect nothing less from her inquisitive son. "Passover has been a part of our family for generations. We take this time to remember what God did when He passed over the houses of the Israelites in Egypt and spared our homes from death. God saw the blood of the lamb over the doorposts of our people. We eat unleavened bread to remind us that He brought us out of bondage and set us apart. Next year, you'll be old enough to go with Papa to bring the lamb for sacrifice."

Thomas's pensive thoughts returned to the present. He packed up the last of his belongings to head out with Jesus and the others. With Passover only six days away, the time had come to leave the wilderness and head toward Jerusalem.

From the Wilderness to the Way

Matthew, Mark, and Luke dedicated a quarter of their Gospels to the last week of Jesus's life. John allotted nearly 50 percent of his gospel to the final events of Jesus's three-year ministry. Jesus knew what this week held for Him . . . a betrayal, a denial, and a trial. More than once throughout the Gospels, He predicted His death, burial, and resurrection. However, even His closest followers did not understand. As He set His face toward the cross, He chose to use His last moments to show the way of faith rather than the way of the world. Jesus never let man-made barriers keep Him from divine appointments. He invited people to come closer no matter what tried to drive them away.

As the sun set across Bethany, Jesus and the apostles returned again, this time for a meal in Jesus's honor. They savored Martha's home-cooked food and joyous conversation. While Lazarus still reclined at dinner, Mary took a jar of expensive perfume, poured it over Jesus's feet, and wiped them with her hair. The aroma of the ointment and her adoration lofted into the room. Before Thomas could even take in the moment, Judas quickly objected to what he deemed a foolish use of money. Jesus silenced the criticism and welcomed her sacrifice. **What some saw as wasteful, He recognized as worship.** "'Leave her alone,' Jesus replied. 'It was intended that she should save this perfume for the day of my burial. You will always have the poor among you, but you will not always have me'" (John 12:7–8).

Jesus's words rang in Thomas's ears . . . "you will not always have me." After a restless night's sleep, Thomas woke to the prospects of a new day. What started as an uneventful journey turned into another opportunity for Jesus to demonstrate His mission. Crowds began to form as Jesus and the apostles reached the outskirts of Jericho. The desperate cries of a blind beggar rose above the clamor: "'Jesus, Son of David, have mercy on me!' Those who led the way rebuked him and told him to be quiet, but he shouted all the more. Jesus stopped and ordered the man to be brought to him (Luke 18:38–40). **What some saw as bothersome, He recognized as brave faith.** Thomas and the others pushed the crowd back and made room for the man to come near. "Jesus asked him, 'What do you want me to do for you?' 'Lord, I want to see,' he replied. Jesus said to him, 'Receive your sight; your faith has healed you.' Immediately he received his sight and followed Jesus, praising God. When all the people saw it, they also praised God (Luke 18:40–43).

Thomas and the apostles struggled to manage the masses. Things only intensified as they reached the heart of town. Zacchaeus, the local chief tax collector, resolved that hatred from others would not deter him from getting a glimpse of Jesus. Unable to see, he climbed a tree for a better vantage point. Jesus told him to come down immediately and headed to his home to visit. **What some saw as reprehensible, He recognized as redeemable.** "Jesus said to him, 'Today salvation has come to this house, because this man, too, is a son of Abraham. For the Son of Man came to seek and to save the lost'" (Luke 19:5–10).

Finally, they entered the city of Jerusalem. The streets bustled with travelers from across the region to celebrate the annual Passover festival. They went out to meet Jesus, waving palm branches to mark His arrival. Thomas and the apostles led Jesus on a colt through the throng of people as shouts of praise rang through the air: "Hosanna! . . . Blessed is the king of Israel!" (John 12:13). The people longed for a deliverer from oppression and interpreted His arrival as the fulfillment of their hopes. On this particular day, the city became thick as families made their way through markets and temple courts to choose their lamb for Passover meal. Jesus entered Jerusalem with intention; He came as the Passover Lamb to take away the sins of the world.

Luke continues in chapter 19:41–42: "As he approached Jerusalem and saw the city, he wept over it and said, 'If you, even you, had only known on this day what would bring you peace—but now it is hidden from your eyes.'" Mere hours later, He revealed sobering news to His closest followers, "My soul is troubled" (John 12:27). The time had come, not for Him to take His place as an earthly king but to lay down His life and be glorified by His Father.

Thomas and the apostles had learned the value of presence and proximity. They continued to stay close to Jesus in the final days of His life on earth. The Gospels of Matthew, Mark,

Luke, and John provide a detailed account of the ways Jesus chose to spend His last week, and Thomas witnessed it all. Jesus continued to contrast the way of the kingdom with the way of the culture. In His first order of business, He drove out those at the temple who were using it for financial gain. By day, He taught and healed there and warned His closest followers of the perilous times to come. By night, He slept on the Mount of Olives nearby. The religious leaders tried to find a way to kill Him, but Luke 19:48 says, "The people hung on his words."

Tensions reached a boiling point in an all-day confrontation. As the Pharisees and members of the Sanhedrin challenged His authority, Jesus revealed the temple would soon be destroyed. While they plotted to arrest Jesus, He prepared to celebrate the Passover meal with His apostles.

All four Gospels share the account of what we refer to as the Lord's Supper. John chapters 13 and 14 contain a series of statements and events that led up to the second time Thomas spoke in Scripture. From the moment they began what would be their last meal together, Thomas and the others could sense that something had shifted. A myriad of emotions flooded Thomas as Jesus took the form of a servant and washed their feet. In a series of startling revelations, He declared that one among them would soon betray Him and that Peter would soon deny Him. The atmosphere grew heavier by the moment. Jesus took the bread and broke it, sharing that His body, too, would be broken for them—and for us. As He took the cup, signifying His blood that would be shed for the salvation of sins, Judas left to conspire with the council against Him.

More than a family conversation over dinner, Jesus's words invited them into a sacred space. Jesus poured out His heart and told them to love one another the way He loved them. He attempted to prepare them for the future with the promise of peace, just as He does for us. We can only imagine what it must have been like for the apostles to sit across from Jesus. However, we often recognize ourselves in their responses. Clouded by confusion and uncertainty, they were unable to accurately process all Jesus shared. He discerned their unsettled hearts, and He sees ours.

In John 14:1–4 Jesus said to them, "Do not let your hearts be troubled. You believe in God; believe also in me. My Father's house has many rooms; if that were not so, would I have told you that I am going there to prepare a place for you? And if I go and prepare a place for you, I will come back and take you to be with me that you also may be where I am. You know the way to the place where I am going."

Thomas could stand it no longer. He had left everything to follow Jesus. The thought of being separated from Jesus without a way to find Him became more than he could bear. Verses 5 and 6 continue, "Thomas said to Him, 'Lord, we don't know where you are going, so how can we know the way?' Jesus answered, 'I am the way and the truth and the life. No one comes to the Father except through me.'"

In the previous encounter, it became imperative for Thomas to go the direction Jesus had chosen. Once he reconciled the cost of his commitment, he spoke to the apostles with firm conviction. In this encounter, Thomas again moved to the forefront, but this time he addressed Jesus. His honest search for answers cut through the silence of the other apostles. Determined to not only know the *place* Jesus intended to go but the *way to get there*, desperation drove Thomas to probe further. He bravely asked two crucial questions that we each need to know the answers to today:

- Where is the place Jesus is going?
- How can I know the way to get there?

Jesus is never afraid of hard questions. As we explore His answer, we will address *the place* in this chapter and examine *the way* in the next.

Troubled or Trusting?

Sensitive to the needs of His closest followers, Jesus took this intimate time to comfort their anxious hearts. With compassion, He encouraged them, "Do not let your hearts be troubled. You believe in God, believe also in me" (John 14:1). He knew that in the coming days, the apostles would experience the most traumatic moments of their lives with Him. They needed the reassurance of the promise of heaven to endure the loss of His presence on earth. Their faith would be tested . . . their courage questioned . . . and they would only stand strong if they believed fully in Him.

Jesus never outlines a problem without a promise. He never gives us a command without the capability and criteria to obey it. We can choose to personalize His promises. Jesus invites us to place our name at the beginning of John chapter 14. "_____, do not let your heart be troubled—put your trust in Me." He knows us and wants an honest, authentic relationship with us. In John 16:33, Jesus makes another promise: "In this world you will have trouble. But take heart! I have overcome the world." We will *have* trouble, but we don't have to *be* troubled. One is an indication of what is around us; the other is an indication of what is within us.

Ours is a finite life in a fallen world. Suffering should not surprise us; it should refine us. We choose whether we walk through life troubled or trusting. This is not our permanent destination; we were created for eternity with Jesus. Billy Graham stated, "My home is in Heaven. I'm just traveling through this world."[2] Eternity is promised for all of us; the question is where we will spend it. The "Father's house" is for everyone who puts their faith in Jesus Christ. Just like the apostles, our hearts are steadied by that promise as we set our hope on things above. And although we can't fully imagine it, Scripture describes the place God's children will one day call home: heaven.

My Father's House

Let's continue in John chapter 14:2–4: "My Father's house has many rooms; if that were not so, would I have told you that I am going there to prepare a place for you? And if I go and prepare a place for you, I will come back to take you to be with me that you also may be where I am. You know the way to the place where I am going."

Most of us have stumbled into that awkward moment where something seemed so clear to someone else but completely muddy to us. Sometimes we just kind of play along, too embarrassed to let on that we don't have a clue. Other times, we have to get clarity to move forward, so we have no choice but to speak up. Thomas found himself in such a conundrum, oblivious to what Jesus stated as the obvious: "You know . . . the place where I am going."

Let's take a moment and normalize what we often feel is an isolated experience: we read the Bible and don't always understand what it means. That's not the time to smile sheepishly and pretend we're good when we're not. We don't have to let shame complicate confusion. We can avail ourselves of the wealth of online resources, the wisdom of seasoned believers, and above all, the help of the Holy Spirit to unpack and apply the truth of God's Word. It is apparent in this and other passages that none of the apostles grasped Jesus's mission, including His death and resurrection. *None* of them knew the way, yet only Thomas became brave enough to speak up. Because he pressed Jesus for more information, they all received greater revelation. This time, he inquired not about direction, but location: "We don't know where are you are going" (John 14:5).

Scriptures throughout the New Testament describe the Father's house as paradise or heaven. Our reference point of home can affect our understanding of the Father's house. For some of us, home evokes the scent of freshly baked chocolate chip cookies . . . the cacophony of voices gathered around fresh pasta at the dinner table . . . the way the ball hit our glove when our dad played catch with us in the front yard. For others, home did not offer a safe place. It represented the sound of raised voices in heated arguments . . . the splintered aftermath of a painful divorce . . . the haunting memories of abuse. God never intended any of this for us. He wants us to know we are fully known and fully loved by Him.

No home is perfect. Whether our home of origin represented a healthy environment or one riddled with heartache, we each long for a place of safety, comfort, and nourishment. Jesus's home, the Father's house, is unlike any home we have ever experienced. In Genesis, we read the account of creation—and all God created "was good." The place Jesus is preparing for us stretches far beyond our comprehension because it is the final perfection that we so desperately long for here on earth.

Jesus added there were many rooms, to ease any concern that it might be full before they got there. Angela says, "Growing up, our family home became filled to the brim on many occasions for ministry gatherings, college get-togethers, and more nights of music than we can count. The memories are priceless. My parents now live in a different home but continue to welcome the next generation of grandchildren and friends. Across thousands of miles, my husband and I practice the hospitality we learned from our parents; our home is a welcome gathering place. Whether in my childhood home, or in our homes now, one constant remains: although we push the limits of our capacity, at some point, the house is full."

Jesus gives us the good news: heaven isn't cramped for space. It offers unlimited vacancy, and it's a place prepared for *you*. Heaven is a personalized, customized place for every single person who believes in Jesus's death and resurrection and who puts their faith in Him.

Who is in Heaven? From beginning to end, the Bible is a love story about the relationship God wants with us. When sin interrupted the fellowship God had with Adam and Eve in the garden, shame and destruction entered the equation. God provided a sacrifice in the garden, and He provided His Son, Jesus, as the atoning sacrifice for our sin. We were created for perfection, but we won't have it this side of eternity. Heaven is the full restoration of all that became ruined by the fall.

Jesus gave the book of Revelation to the apostle John to show what is to come on the earth and what awaits us in heaven. There is no fear, no sickness, no pain, and no tears. It is a place of love, joy, and peace, filled with the presence of God and His people. John tells us that Jesus is seated at the right hand of the Father, receiving glory as the Lamb on the throne. Heaven is marked by His presence. John gives us a glimpse into heaven in Revelation 7:9–10:

> After this I looked, and there before me was a great multitude that no one could count, from every nation, tribe, people and language, standing before the throne and before the Lamb. They were wearing white robes and were holding palm branches in their hands. And they cried out in a loud voice:
>
> > "Salvation belongs to our God,
> > who sits on the throne,
> > and to the Lamb."

If that scene sounds familiar, it should. This is no longer the earthly procession Thomas witnessed as he walked through the dusty streets of ancient Jerusalem. This is King Jesus, the Passover Lamb, slain once and for all for the redemption of mankind. John continues in verse 17,

> For the Lamb at the center of the throne
> > will be their shepherd;
> "he will lead them to springs of living water."
> > "And God will wipe away every tear from
> > their eyes."

Jesus talked extensively about what the kingdom of God is like and who will inherit it. Revelation 21:7 says, "Those who are victorious will inherit all this, and I will be their God and they will be my children." The forgiven are in heaven; Jesus clarified that those who love Him obey His commands. God wants everyone to inherit it, but the choice to receive our inheritance is ours. The apostle Paul writes that heaven is a reward for those who are faithful and a crown of righteousness for those who remain strong until the end. Jesus shares that we must deny ourselves, take up our cross, and follow Him. Denying ourselves means depending on the grace of God to enable us to reject the ways we would disobey Him and His Word. When we embrace surrender, God gives us the endurance to carry our cross. Friend, this isn't easy. We need the constant reminder of heaven.

All things are made new in heaven. In Revelation chapter 21, John shows us a new heaven and a new earth. Our temporary bodies are earthbound and will die, but we will have a new body for eternity. The apostle Paul shares a view of our eternal body in 1 Corinthians chapter 15:51–52, 54–55:

> We will not all sleep, but we will all be changed—in a flash, in the twinkling of an eye, at the last trumpet. For the trumpet will sound, the dead will be raised imperishable, and we will be changed. When the perishable has been clothed with the imperishable, and the mortal with immortality, then the saying that is written will come true: "Death has been swallowed up in victory. Where, O death, is your victory? Where, O death, is your sting?"

When we accept Jesus Christ as our Lord and Savior, we don't need to fear death and the unknown. A. W. Tozer said, "If God takes away from us the old, wrinkled, beat-up dollar bill we have clutched so desperately, it is only because He wants to exchange it for the whole Federal mint, the entire treasury! He is saying to us, 'I have in store for you all the resources of heaven. Help yourself.'"[3]

Who is not in Heaven? Scripture also talks about the alternative to heaven—eternity in hell. It is not an allegory. Hell is a literal place. Jesus spoke several times about hell, warning His followers then and now. He said this in Matthew 13:41–42: "The Son of Man [Jesus] will send out his angels, and they will weed out of his kingdom everything that causes sin and all who do evil. They will throw them into the blazing furnace, where there will be weeping and gnashing of teeth."

God never intended hell for us. He created it for Lucifer (Satan) and his demons who rebelled against God. The Bible says hell is a place of eternal torment and unrelenting regret. If we choose to rebel against God and reject salvation through Jesus Christ, we choose hell as our eternal destination. In Revelation chapter 21:8, John says, "But the cowardly, the unbelieving, the vile, the murderers, the sexually immoral, those who practice magic arts, the idolaters and all liars—they will be consigned to the fiery lake of burning sulfur. This is the second death."

Sin separates us from God and without our acceptance of the atoning sacrifice of His Son, our sin will send us to hell. God does not want anyone to perish. Revelation 21:27 continues, "Nothing impure will ever enter it, nor will anyone who does what is shameful or deceitful, but only those whose names are written in the Lamb's book of life."

Christian apologist Alisa Childers writes this about hell in her compelling book, *Another Gospel?: A Lifelong Christian Seeks Truth in Response to Progressive Christianity*: "We live in a culture in which it is considered arrogant and even hateful to make dogmatic claims about reality. But if we believe the Bible is true—if we follow our Lord Jesus—we must affirm this alongside of Him: Heaven is real. Hell is real. And one day, the door will close."[4]

What does Heaven look like? The clearest picture we have is in Revelation chapter 21:11–12, 18–19, 21–26. John says,

It shone with the glory of God, and its brilliance was like that of a very precious jewel, like a jasper, clear as crystal. It had a great, high wall with twelve gates, and with twelve angels at the gates. The wall was made of jasper, and the city of pure gold, as pure as glass. The foundations of the city walls were decorated with every kind of precious stone. The twelve gates were twelve pearls, each gate made of a single pearl. The great street of the city was of gold, as pure as transparent glass. I did not see a temple in the city, because the Lord God Almighty and the Lamb are its temple. The city does not need the sun or the moon to shine on it, for the glory of God gives it light, and the Lamb is its lamp. The nations will walk by its light, and the kings of the earth will bring their splendor into it. On no day will its gates ever be shut, for there will be no night there. The glory and honor of the nations will be brought into it.

It is not enough just to know that heaven exists, or even to know where it is. We must know the way to get there. Jesus wanted His last conversation with His apostles to point them toward Heaven. The answer Jesus gave to Thomas is the critical answer He gives to us: **"I am the way and the truth and the life. No one comes to the Father except through me"** (John 14:6). That is the ultimate invitation to come closer no matter what tries to drive us away.

As we move forward and explore all that means, let the words of the last chapter of Revelation (22:3–5) bring the comfort our souls crave in these uncertain times:

No longer will there be any curse. The throne of God and of the Lamb will be in the city, and his servants will serve him. They will see his face, and his name will be on their foreheads. There will be no more night. They will not need the light of a lamp or the light of the sun, for the Lord God will give them light. And they will reign for ever and ever.

Up Close with Angela

I am not a morning person. Rolling out of bed while it is still eerily dark constitutes a small miracle. Nonetheless, while in Phoenix, Arizona, for a women's conference in 2008, I became highly motivated to set my alarm for—yawn—4:00 in the morning. The night before, I spotted a brochure in the hotel lobby advertising a glorious way to experience the Sonoran Desert. I couldn't resist the opportunity to do something I had dreamed about for two decades. With the lure of freshly brewed coffee and the promise of adventure, I managed to persuade a dear friend to join me. Throwing caution and common sense to the wind, we headed out to enjoy an exhilarating ride aboard a hot air balloon.

We arrived at the launch site to discover our brightly colored balloon stretched out over the desert floor. After giving us a few safety tips, our guides began inflating it using large tanks filled with propane. I have to admit at this moment, I wondered if a thin sheet of nylon, shooting flames of fire, and a small wicker basket seemed a wise combination, especially considering it would soon be my mode of transportation. "You only live once," I thought. I awkwardly threw my leg over the rim and climbed in.

We lifted off and took flight, propelled only by fire and wind. Within moments, golden and auburn hues filled the Arizona sky as the sun majestically broke over the mountain ridge. It had been a long time since I had watched a sunrise. *Too* long. Loosely directed by our fearless pilot, we began steadily ascending to twelve thousand feet until we were soaring in the open air. Everything looked different. I *felt* different. I breathed deeply, acutely aware of the silence and serenity I had been missing back on the ground. Flying high above the cacti and circumstances, I received an unexpected gift: a transformed perspective.

In Revelation chapter 4, we find John, Jesus's beloved disciple and the author of the book of Revelation, on the island of Patmos. Exiled in a state of incarceration, he literally had nowhere to go but up. On an island of isolation, Jesus extended an invitation to "Come up higher." John experienced the majesty of heaven and the wonder of worship.

"After this I looked, and there before me was a door standing open in heaven. And the voice I had first heard speaking to me like a trumpet said, 'Come up here, and I will show you what must take place after this'" (Revelation 4:1).

Limited by his surroundings, John experienced the unlimited presence of God. We, too, are invited to come up higher—to walk through the door of worship. You may feel isolated on an island of circumstance. Perhaps it seems there is nowhere to go but up. When we get a fresh revelation of who God is, we receive the gift of perspective. If the fear of heights, or just plain sanity, scratches a hot air balloon ride off your list, not to worry. Simply take Jesus's hand and "Come up higher."[5]

Up Close with Hubert

As a young boy, I wanted to be sure that I would go to heaven if I died at that time. I put my confidence in what Jesus did on the cross, trusting that all I needed was for Him to take my place and let His blood be poured out to save me from hell and take me to heaven. It is still the greatest story of sacrificial love that I have ever heard, and I never tire of telling about His love to others.

Throughout the years, many families have asked me to preach funerals for their loved ones. It has been one of my greatest privileges. When their loved one died as a Christian, I have sought to give them wonderful comfort with the scripture that says, "willing rather to be absent from the body, and to be present with the Lord" (2 Corinthians 5:8 KJV). Being present with the Lord means to be in heaven. They are so blessed to be reminded that we are not burying their loved one, but only burying the body, the house they lived in. Regardless of the circumstances surrounding a person's death, I welcome every opportunity to point people to Jesus.

Heaven is still one of the most important subjects to me. Jesus Christ is my Savior, and He promised in the Scriptures to receive me when I die. It is thrilling to think of what will be happening when I get to heaven. It will be breathtaking. I will love taking part in the wonderful singing taking place around the throne of God, offering my worship and gratitude for all Jesus has done to make it possible for me to be there. It is beyond me to say how it will make me feel to look into the face of Jesus. When people looked at Him on earth, His eyes and appearance did not frighten them. Though possessing the power of life and death, He remained gentle with people. He will be approachable in heaven. We will have plenty of time to get close and to speak to Him there.

I will love hearing majestic beings crying out "Holy, holy, holy" (Revelation 4:8) to the Lord God Almighty, Father, Son, and Holy Spirit. It will be amazing to see throngs of angels gathered in awe of what Jesus has done for us Christians. What a wonder it will be to see the millions upon millions of people who trusted in Jesus for everlasting life as they gather and press toward the throne of God.

I can't wait to see Mother and Dad again and many other relatives. It's hard to imagine what a grand reunion we will have, all because Jesus loved us so much. It will be great! I will be forever grateful that my wife joined with me in our stand for Christ in our college years. She saw how I worshipped the Lord Jesus, and she chose me to be her husband. I'm so glad I have served Jesus and have shown that example to my children and grandchildren.

Serving Jesus on earth is preparation for serving Him in heaven. Trusting Him to guide my steps has been exciting and rewarding. I would not trade it for anything. I love what Jesus said about my financial gifts to His kingdom work on the earth. He said, as a result, I have treasures laid up in heaven. It will be interesting to see those treasures.

I am so encouraged by the words of the apostle Paul found in 2 Timothy chapter 4:8: "Now there is in store for me the crown of righteousness, which the Lord, the righteous Judge, will award to me on that day—and not only to me, but also to all who have longed for his appearing." We don't know just what it will look like, but crowns will be given. We read in Revelation 3:11: "Hold on to what you have, so that no one will take your crown."

Let no rebellious thought, word, or deed turn you from obedience to the Savior. Be faithful to follow Jesus and receive the crown that the Lord will have for you. And whether I ever get to meet you in this life, one day, I want to see you in heaven.

Come Closer

Takeaway
My Father's house has many rooms. . . . I go and prepare a place for you. (John 14:2–3)

1. Jesus talked extensively about what the kingdom of God is like and who will inherit it. All things are made new in heaven.
Who and what is in heaven?

2. Scripture also talks about the alternative to heaven—eternity in hell. It is not an allegory. Hell is a literal place. Who is not in heaven?

3. Is there any wonder that Jesus wanted His last conversation with His apostles to point them to heaven?
How strong is your desire to go to heaven?

My prayer in my own words . . .

CHAPTER 7

The Way

Our family traveled to nearly all fifty states, including a summer-long trip through Alaska and the West Coast. Mind you, this took place before GPS devices and Siri were invented to effortlessly guide us on our road trips. Angela recalls, "Whether we were careening around the harrowing curves of the Yukon Territory or traversing the narrow, crowded streets of New York City, one thing stayed constant: we navigated it all with a good, old-fashioned map. To this day, I don't know how my parents did it."

It's one thing to know where you're headed; it's another altogether to know how to get there. Thomas leaned in and listened intently as Jesus answered the first part of his question: "Jesus, where are you going?" Thomas had heard Jesus say, "I will come back and take you to be with me that you also may be where I am" (John 14:3). Perhaps he grappled with the full ramifications of these words—an immortal Jesus would return one day and take us to live with Him forever. Thomas processed the revelation that Jesus, the Son of God, prepared a literal, magnificent, eternal home for him in heaven.

Thomas needed to not only know the destination, but the way to get there. Thomas replied, "Lord, we don't know where you are going, so how can we know the way?" (John 14:5). The answer found in John 14:6 would forever change things for Thomas, and for us: **"I am the way and the truth and the life. No one comes to the Father except through me."** The purpose of the Gospel of John is stated in chapter 20:31: "These [words] are written that you may believe that Jesus is the Messiah." Jesus doesn't just *know* the way, He *is* the way. He doesn't just hold a map; He *is* the map. He is the I AM.

Jesus's central declaration, "I am the way and the truth and the life," is one of seven *I AM* statements in the book of John. In an article entitled, "The 7 'I AM' Statements of Jesus: Old Testament Background and New Testament Meaning," Dustin Crowe writes,

> When God calls Himself the 'I AM' in Exodus 3, it's a pivotal moment in redemptive history. God reveals Himself to His people (Israel) and comes to redeem them out of exile (in Egypt) and lead them into a new life. God's name discloses who He is and what He is like. He is the 'I Am,' the eternal, unchanging, self-existent one, infinite and glorious in every way, and above and beyond all created things. He is God. When Jesus applies the title 'I AM' to himself, He claims to be God—not a helper to God or a great teacher, but the divine, eternal, pre-existent, infinite, perfect Being. He is Israel's God. He is much greater than Moses because He is the God of Moses. He has life in Himself and He can give life to us. The Jews knew taking on this title was making such a claim, which is why they immediately picked up stones to kill him. (John 8:59)[1]

I AM is the claim that Jesus is God. These seven statements confirm His divinity. Thomas and the apostles were with Jesus all seven times He proclaimed Himself as the I AM.

- **I Am the Bread of Life**
  "Then Jesus declared, 'I am the bread of life. Whoever comes to Me will never go hungry, and whoever believes in me will never be thirsty" (John 6:35). This bread is

more than provision for physical hunger. This is a limitless supply of supernatural sustenance. Jesus is represented throughout Scripture as bread and water. We see Him as the miraculous provision of manna in the wilderness for the Israelites. We learn of Him as the showbread in the Tabernacle, the original place of worship. We find Him as the bread celebrated at Passover, representative of His body, broken for the salvation of mankind. We know Him as the water that gushed out of a rock in the desert with Moses and the living water offered to a spiritually malnourished woman at a well in Samaria. He redeemed her and revealed that He is the answer to *our* spiritual hunger and thirst. In John 4:14 Jesus answered her, "Whoever drinks the water I give them will never thirst. Indeed, the water I give them will become in them a spring of water welling up to eternal life."

The crucial point, here, is relationship. Jesus is our source of living bread and living water. Just as we cannot live long without food or water, we cannot live without Him.

- **I Am the Light of the World**
"When Jesus spoke again to the people, he said, 'I am the light of the world. Whoever follows me will never walk in darkness, but will have the light of life'" (John 8:12). We will walk in one of two ways: in light or darkness. It is impossible to find our way or to lead others if we are in darkness. Throughout Scripture, darkness is indicative of spiritual blindness, sinful behavior, and judgment.

In contrast, light is used to describe the Word of God as it illuminates our path in life. In the creation account in the book of Genesis, God "saw that the light was good, and he separated the light from the darkness" (Genesis 1:4). Light invades darkness, and Scripture tells us that the darkness cannot overcome it. Philippians 2:15 says that followers of Christ "May become blameless and pure, 'children of God without fault in a warped and crooked generation.' Then you will shine among them like stars in the sky." In heaven, we will have no need for light because Jesus *is* the light. We cannot find our way without light, and we cannot find our way without Jesus.

- **I Am the Gate to the Sheepfold**
  "I am the gate; whoever enters through me will be saved. They will come in and go out, and find pasture" (John 10:9). The gate is the entry for sheep to go in and find protection or go out and find pasture. If a sheep stays outside the gate, it becomes easy prey. They cannot be left alone without dire consequences—they must have a shepherd. The gate stood as the only way in or out for the sheep. However, they are safe inside the gate under the care of an attentive shepherd. Jesus not only guards the entrance and protects His followers, but He *is* the gate, the only entrance into heaven. We cannot enter the kingdom of God without going through Jesus, the gate.

- **I Am the Good Shepherd**
  "I am the good shepherd; I know my sheep and my sheep know Me—just as the Father knows me and I know the Father—and I lay down my life for the sheep" (John 10:14–15). A shepherd would lay himself down in front of the sheep pen gate to guard the sheep. Even today, a shepherd will search and search for a sheep that becomes separated from the group. Jesus called Himself the Good Shepherd who leaves the ninety-nine to find the one that is lost. He said that His sheep hear His voice. Sheep are lost without a shepherd, and they will only follow the voice of a shepherd they know. If they don't recognize the voice, they will run away in fear. Jesus invites us to remain close enough to Him to know

Him, obey Him, and stay under His care. In Psalm 23:2–3 (KJV) David called God his Shepherd, who "maketh me lie down in green pastures . . . he leadeth me in the paths of righteousness for his name's sake." As our Shepherd, Jesus loves us, protects us, rescues us, and wants a relationship with us. We cannot have guidance and protection without Jesus the Shepherd.

- **I Am the Resurrection, and the Life**
  "Jesus said unto her, I am the resurrection, and the life: he that believeth in me, though he were dead, yet shall he live" (John 11:25 KJV). As we have previously seen, Jesus stated these words to Martha. Jesus wanted Mary and Martha to trust in Him for the answer to every need. Jesus proved Himself to be victorious over death by raising Lazarus from the dead. Jesus restores and raises to new life the areas of our lives that have declined spiritually, mentally, physically, and emotionally. As followers of Christ, we don't need to fear death. When our body reaches the end of its earthly life, Jesus is there. We have no power over death and the grave without Jesus, the resurrection, and the life.

- **I Am the Way, the Truth, and the Life**
  "Jesus answered, 'I am the way and the truth and the life. No one comes to the Father except through Me'" (John 14:6). Jesus set Himself apart from anything that the Jews had previously believed would lead them to God. He *is* what they looked for and needed. He replaced all prior things, such as the temple and system of sacrifices, set up as temporary means by which man related to God. They accomplished only limited things such as making people ceremonially clean. They were never intended to be a long-term solution to sin; they all pointed to Jesus. He alone is able to accomplish our salvation and redemption. He is the only One who

provides the way for us to be reconciled *to* the Father. But He also simultaneously provided the full revelation *of* the Father (truth). There is nowhere else we need to look, or can look, to find the true path to God. We cannot enter heaven through other means; Jesus is the one and only way.

• **I Am the True Vine**
"I am the vine; you are the branches. If you remain in me and I in you, you will bear much fruit; apart from me you can do nothing" (John 15:5). Again, we see the theme of relationship. Our lives will be productive for the kingdom only when we stay connected to Jesus, the Vine, as our source. Jesus called His Father "the vinedresser," and His followers the branches. The apostle Paul, the writer of Philippians 4:13, says that "I can do all this through him who gives us strength." And John 15:5 reminds us that "apart from me you can do nothing" of eternal value. As we abide in Him and His words abide in us, we fulfill what He calls us to be and do in our lifetimes. We cannot do this alone; we need to stay connected to Jesus as our source of life.

The Way

As a young, Jewish man, Thomas received religious training, including how sinners could receive from God the forgiveness of their sins. But it offered only a *temporary* way. This complex system of the Jewish faith included over six hundred laws, the tabernacle in the wilderness, and worship at the temple. Under the first covenant in the Old Testament, the shedding of blood through animal sacrifices provided the necessary atonement for sin. Without that and faith in God, credited to them as righteousness, they could not receive the promise of heaven.

Now, we live under the new covenant, instituted in the New Testament through the death and resurrection of Jesus Christ.

The writer of Hebrews 10:11–13 says,

> Day after day every priest stands and performs his religious duties; again and again he offers the same sacrifices, which can never take away sins. But when this priest [Jesus] had offered for all time one sacrifice for sins, he sat down at the right hand of God, and since that time he waits for his enemies to be made his footstool. For by one sacrifice he has made perfect forever those who are being made holy.

The holy of holies served as the inner chamber of the Jewish temple where only the high priest could enter only once a year. The work of the earthly priest continued year-round, never finished . . . *until Jesus.* At the moment He died on the cross, a violent earthquake shook the ground. The large veil in the temple that barred the entrance to the holy of holies tore from top to bottom—the way opened! Jesus became the *permanent* solution for a humanly, impossible situation.

Throughout history, civilizations have set up man-made constructs and systems to appease "gods" and obtain entrance into "heaven." World religions tell us that there are many ways to heaven: good works, inflicting pain on oneself, being a good person, and offering sacrifices to their own gods. However, no amount of human effort can ever pay our sin debt. Paul writes in Romans 6:23, "For the wages of sin is death, but the gift of God is eternal life in Christ Jesus our Lord." Jesus finished the work of redemption, rescuing us from the bondage of sin by going to the cross and bearing our sins upon Himself. Jesus isn't just *a* way; He is the *only* Way. We accept the free gift of salvation when we confess our sins, receive Jesus as our Savior, and begin a new life through faith in Him.

It is not enough to hear the truth or to know it intellectually. Thomas heard Jesus describe Himself as the only One who could take him and the apostles to the "Father's house." But he had to choose who and what he would believe—and so do we. The realization that we are caught in the trap of sin's penalty and separated from God forever requires a decision: Will we be brave enough to believe in Jesus? He invites us to put our confidence in Him alone to save us and take us to heaven. Thomas received Jesus as more than a guide to give directions for the journey ahead. He believed Jesus to be the Son of God, the Way, the truth, and the life.

Thomas's second question in John 14:5, much more than intellectual pursuit, signified a desperate plea by a devoted follower: "How can we know the way?" He seemed to be saying, "Please don't leave us here without an explanation of where you are going and how to get there. I don't know how to live without you being here with us. I don't feel that I can go on without you here." His simple question provided all the invitation Jesus needed. More than willing, He gladly responded.

Thousands of years later, this is still one of the most important questions we will ever need answered: "How can we know the way to heaven?" We have to understand what Jesus means in John 14:6 when He says, "I am the Way." He doesn't give us a list of things to do to enter heaven: love your spouse, give 10 percent of your income, be kind. Although these are a reflection of a life committed to faith, they are not a punch ticket into heaven. It doesn't work that way. How does it work? Jesus simply says, "I am the way and the truth and the life. No one comes to the Father except through me" (John 14:6).

Many in modern culture hold the view that everyone on earth is a child of God; therefore, everyone receives heaven. But that is not biblically accurate. There is a difference between being *created in the image of God* and *being a child of God*. John 1:12 says, "Yet to all who did receive him; to those who believed in his name, he gave the right to become children of God." We become a child of God when we believe in Jesus and receive Him as the

One who died and took our judgment for sin upon Himself. Heaven is the promised inheritance for the children of God.

The Truth

Jesus revealed more to Thomas than "I am the way." His complex answer included, "I am the truth" (John 14:6). In Colossians 2:9 Paul shares these words, "For in Christ all the fullness of the Deity lives in bodily form." As the second person of the Trinity, Jesus is coequal and coexistent with the Father. Jesus told the apostles that He and God the Father are One, and to know Him is to know the Father.

Dr. Gene A. Getz, author of *The Apostles: Becoming Unified Through Diversity (Men of Character)*, says this about Jesus's declaration, "I am the way and the truth and the life."

> This is one of the most powerful statements in the New Testament. For centuries, men and women have sought to know how to be in contact with the supernatural. The essence of Jesus' whole message was that He was God in human form, and He had come into this world to make this divine contact possible—to provide people with eternal life. He was the Way. Philosophers have also spent a lifetime trying to determine what is really true. Jesus claimed to be—and is—the perfect embodiment of truth. At this point, He was definitely contrasting Himself with Satan, "who was a murderer from the beginning, not holding to the truth."[2]

The study of biblical truth is a fascinating one. The apostle John, under the inspiration of the Holy Spirit, wrote this in chapter 1:14, "And the Word was made flesh, and dwelt among us, (and we beheld his glory as of the only begotten of the Father,) full of grace and truth." Jesus was full of truth, the transparent revelation of God. In Him, there is nothing deceitful and nothing false. John 1:17 says, "For the law was given through

Moses, but grace and truth came through Jesus Christ." Jesus is not a subjective interpretation of truth; He is *the truth*. He is the objective standard by which all other "truth" must be measured.

In "Up Close with Angela" at the end of this chapter, we share excerpts from a riveting conversation between Angela and Dr. George Barna. In his startling new research, statistics show that the majority of Americans determine what they believe by interpreting the world through the filter of their feelings and experiences rather than through the Bible. The idea of *speaking my truth* is flawed because "our truth" is subjective, based on our perceptions, limited understanding, and cognitive bias. We do have an absolute standard for truth—the Bible and the person of Jesus Christ. Truth is not relative. **If *our* truth contradicts *the* truth, it is not truth.** We must confront and challenge any false beliefs we may hold. We must also resist the lies from Satan that set themselves up against the truth of God's Word. John 8:32 says, "Then you will know the truth, and the truth will set you free." Truth, in the person of Jesus Christ, sets us free from deception and free from the Deceiver.

The Spirit of Truth

Thomas and the other apostles struggled with the thought that they would be left alone without Jesus's physical presence. Jesus sought to alleviate their concern by teaching them about the Holy Spirit, the Spirit of Truth, who would come to them after His ascension to heaven. John 14:18 says, "I will not leave you as orphans; I will come to you." He would always be with them —and with us—in the person of the Holy Spirit.

In John 14:15–17 He shared, "If you love me, keep my commands. And I will ask the Father, and he will give you another advocate to help you and be with you forever—the Spirit of truth." He continued in verses 26–27, "But the Advocate, the Holy Spirit, whom the Father will send in my name, will teach you all things and will remind you of everything I have said to you. Peace I leave with you; my peace I give you. I do not give to you as the world gives. Do not let your hearts be troubled and do not be afraid."

The Holy Spirit, the third person of the Trinity, enables and empowers us to live without fear. We are never alone. In John 16:6–7 Jesus shared, "Rather, you are filled with grief because I have said these things. But very truly I tell you, it is for your good that I am going away. Unless I go away, the Advocate will not come to you; but if I go, I will send him to you." Verses 13–14 state, "When he, the Spirit of truth, comes, he will guide you into all the truth. He will not speak on his own; he will speak only what he hears, and he will tell you what is yet to come. He will glorify me because it is from me that he will receive what he will make known to you."

At salvation, the Holy Spirit—the Spirit of God—lives inside of us. Scripture tells us we are the temple or the dwelling place of the Holy Spirit. He helps us to understand and apply the truth of God's Word. He is involved in the daily events of our lives, giving us the will of God even when we don't know He is doing it. We will discuss His crucial role more in our last chapter.

The Life

It was not enough for Jesus to answer Thomas with the words, "I am the way and the truth." With a resounding exclamation mark, He also declared, "I am the life." Three of the *I AM* statements that Jesus made about Himself specifically mention life: "I am the bread of life, I am the resurrection and the life, and I am the way and the truth and the life." Why such an emphasis on life? God's original intent at creation was that we would live forever. However, with the fall of mankind came the curse of sin, decay, and death. Death came through the work of Satan, while life came through the work of Jesus. Jesus restored what was lost in the garden of Eden.

In 1 John 5:12 we read, "Whoever has the Son has life; whoever does not have the Son of God does not have the life." Jesus is the unlimited, inexhaustible source of our abundant life on earth and our eternal life in heaven. After a radical transformation, the apostle Paul was marked by the power of grace. He possessed a profound awareness of the life he now lived through faith in Jesus Christ. Under the inspiration of the Holy Spirit, Paul wrote several books of the New Testament. Look at the way His words help us grasp the abundant life we have been given through Christ:

- The promise of life . . .
  "Paul, an apostle of Christ Jesus by the will of God, in keeping with the promise of life that is in Jesus Christ" (2 Timothy 1:1).
- The spirit of life . . .
  "Because through Christ Jesus the law of the Spirit who gives you life has set you free from the law of sin and of death" (Romans 8:2).
- The faith-fueled life . . .
  "I have been crucified with Christ and I no longer live, but Christ lives in me. The life I now live in the body, I live by faith in the Son of God, who loved me and gave himself for me" (Galatians 2:20).
- The fully-surrendered life . . .
  "For to me, to live is Christ and to die is gain" (Philippians 1:21).
- The life to come . . .
  "When Christ, who is your life, appears, then you also will appear with him in glory" (Colossians 3:4).

In 1 Corinthians 15:26 (KJV), Paul says, "The last enemy to be destroyed is death." Jesus, victorious over the grave, canceled the curse of sin and death. John 10:10 (KJV) tells us, "The thief cometh not, but for to steal, and to kill, and to destroy: I am come that they might have life, and that they might have it more abundantly."

Thomas may have felt anxious about death or wondered when Jesus would take him to be with Him in heaven. He may have thought it would be sometime far beyond death. He did not have Paul's words in 2 Corinthians 5:8: "We are confident, I say, and would prefer to be away from the body and at home with the Lord." There is no space in time between the moment we leave this body and go into the presence of the Lord. We see this in Luke chapter 23 as we read the story of two criminals who were crucified on each side of Jesus Christ. One hurled insults while the other asked Jesus to remember him when He came into His kingdom. We read in verse 43: "Jesus answered him, 'Truly I tell you, today, you will be with me in paradise.'" If the other criminal had also called upon Jesus to save him, he too, would have inherited eternal life.

We were created for eternity—it is just a matter of *where* we will spend it. When we place our faith in Jesus Christ, death is not the end; it is the beginning of eternity in heaven. He says to us, "When your body can no longer take care of you, I will take care of you now." God was unwilling to leave us in a helpless, hopeless condition. Through Jesus, everything that is now broken will one day be made whole. We have the certain promise of heaven in this uncertain place called earth. In a world that is deeply fractured by sin and heartache, we have the hope of eternal life.

The Way Home

When Thomas pressed Jesus for the answers he desperately needed, he did not understand that it represented the last conversation he would have with Him before Jesus went to the cross. That evening, Thomas and the apostles followed Jesus into the garden of Gethsemane. Knowing what lay before Him, Jesus asked the Father if there might be *any other way* mankind could be brought into fellowship with Him. As He prayed, drops of blood fell from His brow. Deep anguish gave way to complete surrender. "Father, if you are willing, take this cup from me; yet not my will, but yours be done" (Luke 22:42).

With no other way to provide salvation for us, Jesus *became the Way*. Our last encounter between Thomas and Jesus reveals how that makes all the difference, not just for a beloved disciple in his darkest moment of despair, but for us. He is the Way when we feel crushed by the injustice of a situation. He is the Way when we feel overwhelmed by our circumstances. He is the Way when we feel bruised by doubt and battered by disappointment. He is the Way when we can't find our footing and don't know our next steps. He is the Way when we don't have the strength to try again. He is the Way to life.

We don't have to traverse the agonizing curves of life alone. When we are brave enough to believe in Jesus Christ, we aren't handed a paper map or even the most sophisticated navigational system to get through life. We are given the love of our Heavenly Father, the infallible Word of God, the power of the Holy Spirit, and the promise that heaven will one day be our home.

Up Close with Angela

Dr. George Barna is often called "the most quoted person in the Christian Church today."[3] He is a professor at Arizona Christian University and the director of research at the Cultural Research Center at ACU. He is also a fellow at the Townsend Institute, has taught at the undergraduate and graduate level, and has pastored two churches. He founded the Barna Group, a research company that for years set the standard for understanding trends in American culture. He is the author of more than fifty books, including numerous award winners and *New York Times* bestsellers. His recent research, *The American Worldview Inventory* revealed that just 6% of U.S. adults possess a biblical worldview. In Episode 94 of the *Make Life Matter* podcast, "God's Truth or My Truth," I sat down with Dr. Barna to discuss the opportunities emerging from the pandemic, the cut-and-paste approach most Americans take to making sense of life, and how we can move the needle toward thoughtful dependence on the Bible to frame our worldview. The most common worldview might best be described as syncretism, a disparate, irreconcilable collection of beliefs and behaviors that define our lives.

Everybody has a worldview. We need a worldview to get through the day. It is essentially the intellectual, emotional, spiritual filter that you use to experience and interpret and respond to the world. It's the filter through which you make every decision that you make—it's critical. Part of Jesus's ministry was to say, let's not take what Rome says, or what the Sanhedrin says, or what anyone says is right or proper or appropriate for you, because ultimately the God of the universe made you, loves you, and has a plan and purpose for your life. But to fulfill it, you've got to think carefully about who you are, how you're going to live, and how you're going to interact with all these other philosophies of life (for example. other worldviews.) Syncretism indicates that there are many different worldviews that a person can choose from. A Biblical worldview is simply going back to the Bible and figuring out what are the main principles and commands and ideas contained in it that God gives to us so that we can live a life that not only pleases and glorifies and honors Him, but it enables us to thrive here on earth.

There are more than a dozen worldviews that Americans are exposed to regularly and that they draw from. They will grab onto an idea from Marxism. Then they will grab onto an idea they kind of like from secular humanism. Then they will hear something that Eastern mysticism proposes and they say, wow, I want that to be part of my worldview. And before you know it, they have all these different disparate ideas that they've molded together into this "cut-and-paste" idea. Roughly 9 out of 10 have this bizarre mixture of beliefs, and we don't challenge the contradictions. We're just trying to feel good about ourselves and get through the day, and if it doesn't work we will try something else the next time. In our culture today, we don't take worldviews seriously enough to say, when you're a child, we're going to intentionally and strategically focus on developing your worldview.

The most effective means of facilitating transformation in others' lives is through mentoring. Someone who is more mature than me reaches back to me and helps me progress in my walk with Christ. We need to bring people together today and look at the preaching and teaching in the Church today. We can't avoid the basics. We need to hear God's truth based on where we are at in our lives to continually challenge us to be more Christlike."[4]

Jesus's words are clear: He is the only Way. Our culture continues to formulate its own truth and accept other ways to be reconciled to the Father. Jesus Himself settled the question once and for all in the garden. If there had been another way, God would have allowed for it. We hold Jesus's death and resurrection as a non-negotiable truth of the Christian faith. As our one and only Mediator, Jesus is the one and only Way.

Up Close with Hubert

When I served for two years as a North Carolina state youth director, I asked for teenagers from several churches to volunteer and join me in Wilson, North Carolina, for a Saturday evangelism outreach. The young people and I gathered at a church facility where I gave them instructions about the way we would approach a home and begin a conversation. We asked for God's help and went house to house with one objective: let people know we would like to talk with them about Jesus and what He meant to us.

One of the young men and I knocked on a door where an elderly man invited us to come in. As we visited together, we realized he wanted to be sure his sins were forgiven. We sensed his readiness to receive Jesus as his Savior. We saw his eyes light up as we talked about the many times God showed His love and care for him. He expressed his gratitude for the years God had given him to live. We explained how Jesus died in his place to satisfy the justice of God and provide him the way of peace with God and everlasting life. We told him the words of Jesus found in the Bible in Revelation 3:20, "I stand at the door and knock. If anyone hears my voice and opens the door, I will come in and eat with that person, and they with me." He listened and he made his choice to have us pray with him for the salvation of his soul. He expressed his faith in Jesus Christ and his desire to do God's will. After we prayed, it became evident that a great load was lifted off him. He became confident that he had chosen the right way to heaven.

That experience made a profound impact on me and the young man who accompanied me to that home. He devoted himself to become a caring pastor who has influenced many others to open their hearts to Christ and receive the assurance of eternal life. What can be more important than inviting someone to receive Jesus as their personal Savior? What an adventure! Enjoy the journey!

Come Closer

Takeaway

I am the way and the truth and the life. No one comes to the Father except through me. (John 14:6)

1. The 7 "I AM" Statements of Jesus reveal His divine nature: The Bread of Life, The Light of the World, The Gate, The Good Shepherd, The Resurrection and the Life, The Way, the Truth, and the Life, and The True Vine.
Which of these statements revealing Jesus's character mean the most to you at this moment in your life?

2. It is not enough to hear the truth or to know it intellectually. Thomas heard Jesus describe Himself as the only One who could take him and the apostles to the "Father's house."
Why is it absolutely essential to receive Jesus and believe He is the one and only Way to Heaven?

3. God was unwilling to leave us in a helpless, hopeless condition. Through Jesus, everything that is now broken will one day be made whole.

How do these two chapters on the promise of Heaven reassure our fragile hearts that death is not the end but the beginning of eternity with Jesus?

My prayer in my own words . . .

ENCOUNTER 4

CHAPTER 8

Absence

Under the cover of darkness, Jesus led Thomas and the apostles to the olive grove nearby where He often went to pray. The garden of Gethsemane became the last place Thomas saw Jesus alive. In these familiar surroundings, His closest followers, those who walked with Him, ate with Him, learned from Him, and loved Him, abandoned Him in fear. Yet, in the void left by the apostles, we see how God writes *every one of us* into this story.

Over the next twenty-four hours, Jesus would be betrayed, put on trial, crucified, and buried... with Thomas conspicuously absent. He can't give us an eyewitness account of these events that changed history, but he can give us a front-row seat to grace. In his story, we catch glimpses of our own. Desperate moments can cause us to become painfully aware of our vulnerability. We, too, can retreat to hiding places when fear crowds out faith. Jesus knows just where to find us and invites us to come closer no matter what tries to drive us away.

The Garden

All four Gospels record the final events of Jesus's earthly life. In Mark 14:32–37, 41–42 we are told,

> They went to a place called Gethsemane, and Jesus said to his disciples, "Sit here while I pray." He took Peter, James and

John along with him, and he began to be deeply distressed and troubled. "My soul is overwhelmed with sorrow to the point of death," he said to them. "Stay here and keep watch." Going a little farther, he fell to the ground and prayed that if possible the hour might pass from him. "*Abba*, Father," he said, "everything is possible for you. Take this cup from me. Yet not what I will, but what you will." Then he returned to his disciples and found them sleeping, "Simon," he said to Peter, "are you asleep? Couldn't you keep watch for one hour?" Returning the third time, he said to them, "Are you still sleeping and resting? Enough! The hour has come. Look, the Son of Man is delivered into the hands of sinners. Rise! Let us go! Here comes my betrayer!"

Despite multiple requests from Jesus, they could not stay awake. While He fell to the ground in agony, they fell asleep. This marks the beginning of their absence during Jesus's most critical moments. The apostles did not assess the gravity of the situation. We, too, can find ourselves spiritually asleep to the times we are living in. If we become aloof to the condition of our culture, apathy and absence can follow. The Enemy wants us to disengage from our faith community and miss meaningful moments for the kingdom. Jesus asks us the same question He asked Thomas and the apostles: "Will we not stay awake and pray?"

Although their actions don't reflect it, the apostles had been made aware of the burden Jesus carried. How can we know that for sure? First, Jesus repeatedly tried to prepare them for what would come. He foretold His betrayal, death, and resurrection. Even at the Lord's Supper, Jesus shared about this moment in the garden. Matthew 26:23–25 says,

> Jesus replied, "The one who has dipped his hand into the
> bowl with me will betray me. The Son of Man will go just as
> it is written about him. But woe to the man who betrays the

Son of Man! It would be better for him if he had not been born." Then Judas, the one who would betray him, said, "Surely you don't mean me, Rabbi?" Jesus answered, "You have said so."

Second, God continually sought to prepare His people concerning future events about the coming Messiah through the message of the prophets. "The story of Jesus saturates the metanarrative of the Bible, and prophecies of His first advent are found throughout the Old Testament. Allusions to Him also come up in micro ways, as many people and events hint at the work He would accomplish. One scholar, J. Barton Payne, has found as many as 574 verses in the Old Testament that somehow point to or describe or reference the coming Messiah. Alfred Edersheim found 456 Old Testament verses referring to the Messiah or His times. Conservatively, Jesus fulfilled at least 300 prophecies in His earthly ministry."[1]

Thomas and the apostles would have known about the prophecies given and recorded hundreds of years earlier, fulfilled through Jesus Christ. Even the wicked King Herod at the time of Jesus's birth asked the scribes and teachers of the day to tell him "where the Messiah was to be born" (Matthew 2:4). The apostles are absent from Jesus's final moments, but the fulfillment of prophecy is not. We have no shortage of evidence that Jesus is who He says He is. For those brave enough to believe, this provides the assurance of His divinity, sent from the Father as "the Lamb of God, who takes away the sin of the world!" (John 1:29).

From a place of crushing in an olive grove to the place of the skull, Golgotha, we include only a handful of the several hundred prophecies concerning Jesus. Through Jesus's betrayal, trial, crucifixion, and resurrection, we see prophecies fulfilled. A thousand years before the birth of Jesus, David prophesied about Jesus's betrayal. His words in Psalm 41:9 reveal it:

Even my close friend
someone I trusted,
one who shared my bread,
has turned against me.

John 18:2–3 says, "Now Judas, who betrayed him, knew the place, because Jesus had often met there with his disciples. So Judas came to the garden, guiding a detachment of soldiers and some officials from the chief priests and the Pharisees. They were carrying torches, lanterns and weapons."

Not knowing what to expect, the soldiers came prepared for a fight. Yet, Judas wielded the greatest weapon—his selfish will against God. We weaponize our will when we choose disobedience and rebellion against the things of God. Judas's choices stemmed from his desire for a certain kind of deliverer, a warrior who would show power and authority against the Romans. Judas couldn't accept Jesus as the compassionate Lamb of God; he only wanted Him to be the conquering Lion of Judah.

Mark 14:44 says, "Now the betrayer had arranged a signal with them: 'The one I kiss is the man; arrest him and lead him away under guard.'" Hundreds of years earlier, the psalmist penned these words about the coming Messiah in Psalm 2:12, "Kiss his son." Throughout the New Testament, the word *proskuneo* is used to describe worship. "According to Strong's Concordance "proskuneo" means "to kiss" as in to kiss the hand of a superior. It is commonly associated with bowing down or lying prostrate on the ground with the idea of kissing the ground before someone."[2]

Why did Judas betray Jesus with a kiss? Judas traveled with Thomas and the apostles, receiving the full revelation of Jesus's ministry. Judas looked to Jesus as his Rabbi and teacher, a position of great reverence and respect. He would have grasped the symbolism and significance of greeting Jesus with a kiss. Many theologians believe that Judas hoped his act would incite a nonviolent Jesus to start a rebellion against the Romans. However, Jesus would not be manipulated.

We find in the Gospel of Luke, chapter 22:49–51: "When Jesus' followers saw what was going to happen, they said, 'Lord, should we strike with our swords?' And one of them [Simon Peter] struck the servant of the high priest, cutting off his right ear. But Jesus answered, 'No more of this!' And He touched the man's ear and healed him."

Judas betrayed Jesus, and moments later, Peter resorted to defense of Jesus. Thomas observed the ways in which Jesus refused to allow anything, or anyone, to take Him off course from His mission. Look at Jesus's words in Matthew 26:55–56. "In that hour Jesus said to the crowd, 'Am I leading a rebellion, that you have come out with swords and clubs to capture me? Every day I sat in the temple courts teaching, and you did not arrest me. But this has all taken place that the writings of the prophets might be fulfilled." Our Heavenly Father not only provided Jesus as the Way for our salvation, but He planned the *specific* ways in which each detail of our redemption would unfold.

In Matthew 26:31, Jesus told His apostles, "This very night you will all fall away on account of me, for it is written: 'I will strike the shepherd, and the sheep of the flock will be scattered.'" Six hundred thirty years before the time of Jesus's birth, Zechariah prophesied about the way the events would take place in the garden. Zechariah 13:7 says, "Strike the shepherd, and the sheep will be scattered." Matthew 26:56 confirms precisely what happened, "Then all the disciples deserted him and fled."

Their fear of arrest turned to absence. Terrified, Thomas and the apostles ran for their lives. We can only imagine how Thomas's heartbeat throbbed in his ears as he frantically made his way out of the guard's grasp and into the anonymity of the night air. This is Thomas who previously led the apostles with a bold charge, "Let us also go, that we may die with him" (John 11:16). This is Thomas who received the assurance of a home prepared for those who believe. Fear is a powerful motivator. The apostles were aware of what would soon happen to Jesus, but that alone proved not enough. When the moment came, they abandoned Him. Except for John who stayed faithfully by the cross of Christ, Thomas and the other apostles are completely absent from the gospel narrative until after the resurrection.

The Trial

Accompanied by the brute force of the Roman guards to bolster their charge, the Jewish leaders arrested Jesus and brought Him before the court of the Sanhedrin. With the great I AM present, the final confrontation occurred between Jesus and the Jewish council. The chief priests and teachers of Jewish law sought any evidence they might find to convict Jesus of a crime. They settled upon His answer to this question, posed in Mark's Gospel, chapter 14:61, "Are you the Messiah, the Son of the Blessed One?"

"'I am,' said Jesus. 'And you will see the Son of Man sitting at the right hand of the Mighty One and coming on the clouds of heaven'" (Mark 14:62).

The Council would have immediately recognized His words, first recorded by the prophet Daniel in chapter 7:13–14:

> In my vision at night I looked, and there before me was one like a son of man, coming with the clouds of heaven. He approached the Ancient of Days and was led into his presence. He was given authority, glory, and sovereign power; all nations and peoples of every language worshiped him. His dominion is an everlasting dominion that will not pass away, and his kingdom is one that will never be destroyed.

The high priest pronounced Jesus's claim as blasphemy. In this sham of a trial which broke several Jewish laws, he condemned Jesus as worthy of death. Mark 14:65 continues, "Then some began to spit at him; they blindfolded him, struck him with their fists, and said, 'Prophesy!' And the guards took him and beat him."

No doubt, there were those in the crowd who remembered the psalmist's words found in Psalm 22:7: "All who see me mock me; they hurl insults, shaking their heads." They were witnessing the fulfillment of prophecy given hundreds of years before. Having no authority to execute Jesus, they took Him to Pilate, the Roman governor over the area. Finding no fault in Him, he released Jesus to the Jews who took Him to King Herod. King Herod questioned Jesus and returned Him to the rightful authority in the matter, Pilate. John chapters 18 and 19 record a lengthy conversation between Pilate and Jesus. Distraught over Jesus's innocence, Pilate ordered Jesus flogged to appease the Jews. In John 19:9–11, Pilate pulled Jesus back inside the palace to speak to Him once again in private.

> "Where do you come from?" he asked Jesus, but Jesus gave him no answer.
>
> "Do you refuse to speak to me?" Pilate said. "Don't you realize I have power either to free you or to crucify you?"
>
> Jesus answered, "You would have no power over me if it were not given to you from above. Therefore the one who handed me over to you is guilty of a greater sin."

Under strong political pressure and great duress, Pilate ordered Jesus to be crucified. Throughout history, and still today, God uses those in authority to fulfill what He has planned for the redemption of mankind. God worked through the Jewish religious rulers, an ambivalent governor, a wicked king, and Roman soldiers to fulfill prophecy and accomplish His will. We can confidently trust that God is in control of circumstances, events that shape history, and time itself. That does not mean we don't pray and seek God for His kingdom to come on earth as it is in heaven. We can be brave enough to believe that God is on the throne and hears our prayers. His plans will overrule others.

Those given earthly authority over Jesus subjected Him to intense interrogation. Although they listened carefully to His answers, they refused to accept what He said as truth or receive Him as the promised Messiah. Today, Jesus is still placed on trial in the hearts and minds of some who wrestle with the same questions posed two thousand years ago:

- Is Jesus the Messiah, the Son of God?
- What do I do with Jesus?

The answers we give will determine our destiny.

The Cross

Crucifixion was a public execution. Those sentenced to death were required to carry their cross through the congested streets of Jerusalem, strewn with markets and animals. As Jesus carried His cross down the Via Dolorosa or "Way of Suffering," He collapsed under the weight of it. Luke chapter 23 tells us that soldiers seized Simon of Cyrene and forced him to carry it the remainder of the way. Because Jesus's disciples were absent, this sacred assignment fell to a stranger just passing by. We can be quick to judge them for deserting Him. Yet, our commitment can wane when the cost of following Jesus becomes too great. We can be tempted to distance ourselves from Him when we bear the bruise of disappointment instead of the cross He calls us to carry.

The prophet Isaiah tells us that Jesus became disfigured beyond recognition. Even still, there were those in the crowd who knew He had healed them . . . delivered them . . . and freed them from their suffering. Now *He* was becoming the suffering servant for them—and for us.

Others nearby barely glanced in His direction. They saw nothing more than another condemned criminal on another ordinary day. *Except He wasn't.* The spotless, sinless Son of God became flesh and lived among us. And on this day, the God of the universe surrendered His life for our salvation. No one pushed Jesus down on a cross. He laid down willingly through the power of love. Jesus said in John 10:17–18, "The reason my Father loves me is that I lay down my life—only to take it up again. No one takes it from me, but I lay it down of my own accord. I have authority to lay it down and authority to take it up again."

Metal split wood as nails were driven into Jesus's hands and feet. Roman soldiers were unaware that they, too, were a part of the fulfillment of prophecies written hundreds of years before they were born. They would not have known or studied the writings of the Old Testament. As they put Jesus on the cross, they decided to take His clothes and divide them amongst themselves. When one seamless garment remained, John 19:24 tells us they said, "Let's not tear it . . . Let's decide by lot who will get it." Psalm 22:18 says, "They divide my clothes among them and cast lots for my garment."

They lifted the cross that held the Savior toward heaven and thrust it into the ground. Some who witnessed His crucifixion raised their voices and shouted a chorus of jeers while others bowed their heads and wept in deep sorrow. Even these moments of intense personal anguish for Jesus were saturated with love. He had words to say to those closest to Him, those crucified next to Him, and His Father in heaven. The apostle John writes in chapter 19:25–27, "Near the cross of Jesus stood His mother, his mother's sister, Mary the wife of Clopas, and Mary Magdalene. When Jesus saw His mother there, and the disciple whom He loved [John] standing nearby, he said to her, 'Woman, here is your son,' and to the disciple, 'Here is your mother.' From that time on, this disciple took her into his home."

Jesus remained fully aware of everything happening to Him and around Him. He pardoned the repentant thief on the cross and told him that he would be with Him in paradise. And He prayed for those who crucified Him, "Father, forgive them, for they know not what they are doing" (Luke 23:34).

Matthew chapter 27:46 says, "About three in the afternoon Jesus cried out in a loud voice, '*Eli, Eli, lema sabachthani?*' (which means 'My God, my God, why have you forsaken me?')" David wrote about this painful moment of separation in Psalm 22:1, "My God, my God, why have you forsaken me?" As Jesus, who knew no sin, became sin for us, the Father turned His face away from His Son. God is holy; no sin can enter His presence. Jesus knew all it would cost Him, yet He finished the work of redemption at the cross.

The apostle John includes two additional prophecies fulfilled by the Roman guards. To expedite the process of death, soldiers customarily broke the legs of those being crucified. The soldiers broke the legs of one of the thieves hanging next to Jesus. However, John 19:33–34 says, "But when they came to Jesus and found that he was already dead, they did not break his legs. Instead, one of the soldiers pierced Jesus's side with a spear, bringing a sudden flow of blood and water." God had revealed His will to the psalmist in chapter 34:20, "He protects all his bones, not one of them will be broken." Zachariah 12:10 says, "And I will pour out on the house of David and the inhabitants of Jerusalem a spirit of grace and supplication. They will look on me, the one they have pierced, and they will mourn for him."

In Luke 23:46 we read, "Jesus called out with a loud voice, 'Father, into your hands I commit my spirit.' When he had said this, he breathed his last." This fulfilled the words of the psalmist in Psalm 31:5: "Into your hands I commit my spirit; deliver me, LORD, my faithful God." At that moment, darkness engulfed the hill of Golgotha and the curtain in the temple tore from top to bottom. God opened the Way for anyone who believed in Jesus to have direct access into His presence. As an earthquake shook the ground, the Roman soldiers at the foot of the cross realized they had experienced a divine encounter. Matthew 27:54 tells us, "When the centurion and those with him who were guarding Jesus saw the earthquake and all that had happened, they were terrified, and exclaimed, 'Surely he was the Son of God!'"

On a wooden cross, Jesus bore the sins of the entire world. We could never bridge the distance sin created between us and God. But God, the righteous judge, wrote: "*You are forgiven*" in letters stained red by the blood of Jesus. When we are brave enough to believe in Jesus as our Savior, God no longer sees us covered by sin and shame but righteous and redeemed through His Son.

The Burial

In the absence of the apostles, two secret converts of Jesus took His body and prepared Him for burial. John 19:38–39 says, "Joseph of Arimathea asked Pilate for the body of Jesus. Now Joseph was a disciple of Jesus, but secretly because he feared the Jewish leaders. With Pilate's permission, he came and took the body away. He was accompanied by Nicodemus, the man who earlier had visited Jesus at night." Per Jewish burial rites, they brought myrrh, aloes, and linen to wrap His body and laid Him in a new tomb in a nearby garden.

From the moment Thomas and the apostles fled the scene at Jesus's arrest to the deafening silence that followed the sealed tomb, shame robbed them of peace. Perhaps they wondered how this had happened. In their absence, we are left with a question of our own. How is it possible that they are missing from the narrative of the most meaningful moments in Jesus's life?

We want a neat, tidy story, one where everyone is right where they are supposed to be. We think we should read the version where Simon Peter and Andrew are close enough to Jesus to carry His cross ... where Thomas and Matthew quiet the insults from the crowd ... and James and John wrap His broken, bloody body and bury their Master. But instead, we sit with discomfort as we read about Simon the Cyrene, a condemned thief, and

Joseph of Arimathea and Nicodemus, two men too afraid to acknowledge their faith in Jesus Christ.

We think to ourselves, surely, this can't be right. This must be a mistake. The Gospel doesn't make any mistakes, but it does make us uncomfortable. And it invites us in. Through the encounters present in the final hours of Jesus's earthly life, we see the heart of our Heavenly Father. A common criminal, who had nothing to offer Jesus, received forgiveness moments before his death. A Roman soldier, an enemy of Jesus, praised God and acknowledged Jesus as the Son of God. Two Jewish leaders, covert believers, were entrusted to care for the Savior of the world.

Can you see it? **In the apostles' absence, God wrote all of humanity into this story.**

We tend to read the Bible through a lens of what it says to and about us. But the Bible is to be read, first and foremost, as a revelation of what it says about God. Scripture is the way we know who He is *and* how we are included in His story. With this lens, we are no longer heartbroken as we think of Jesus being without His closest friends. Instead, we are overwhelmed by His love to die for a stranger, for an enemy, for a criminal, and for those afraid to admit they followed Him. They were drawn by this invitation: come closer and be brave enough to believe. The apostles spent years with Jesus, while each of these only had Him for a moment. But when you encounter Jesus, a moment is enough.

Perhaps you have found yourself in this story . . .

- Like Simon of Cyrene, Jesus has been little more than a stranger to you as you go about your everyday life. Jesus is inviting you closer.
- Or, like the thief on the cross, you feel that you've wasted time and have nothing to offer Jesus. Jesus is inviting you closer.

- You may see your reflection in the Roman soldier as you look at your choices and lament what you have done. Jesus is inviting you closer.
- Perhaps fear has shrouded your belief in Jesus Christ, and you've kept Him a secret because of what others might say. Jesus is inviting you closer.

Jesus's betrayal, trial, death, and burial were not a haphazard string of unfortunate events. God divinely orchestrated every moment for our salvation. John 3:16 (KJV) tells us, "For God so loved the world, that he gave his only begotten Son, that whosoever believeth in him should not perish, but have everlasting life." Jesus is in it all and over it all. He doesn't just invite His closest friends to know Him, He invites *the whosoever*—the wanderer, the wondering, and the wayward. He invites us all.

The Resurrection

The news began to travel: Jesus was dead. As hours stretched into days, Thomas and the apostles stayed out of sight from the Jewish leaders and out of reach from the Roman guards. However, they would soon discover that death would not have the final word.

Early on the third day, before dawn had even announced its arrival, Mary Magdalene gathered both her belongings and her bruised emotions to make her way to the tomb. As she neared the entrance, her breath caught in the back of her throat: the stone had been rolled away. Her heart pounded and her thoughts raced . . . Who would do this? Who would come and steal His body? Immediately, she left to tell Peter and John. Rushing back to the tomb where Jesus's body had been placed, Peter was the first to enter the empty tomb. Sunlight streamed into the dimly lit tomb. As his eyes adjusted, a shape began to take form. In place of Jesus's body, only the grave clothes remained. They went back to where they were staying, but Mary lingered at the empty tomb. It was all too much. Mary was undone.

"Why are you crying? Who are you looking for?"

Mary turned to the voice behind her. Thinking he was the gardener, she pleaded, "Sir, if you have carried him away, tell me where you have put him, and I will get him."

Jesus said to her, "Mary."

Standing in front of her was the resurrected Christ. *Jesus had risen!*

Jesus told Mary to deliver the message to the others: He was alive. With every step, memories flooded her mind. Jesus had rescued her from a life of sin and shame. He had delivered her from multiple demons that held her hostage. He had welcomed her into His inner circle of closest friends. And now, He had appeared to her—first—after His resurrection. She had been desperate for redemption. Now, she had been chosen for revelation.

Face-to-face with the apostles, she exclaimed, "I have seen the Lord" (John 20:18). Later that evening, John 20:19–22, 24 says,

> When the disciples were together, with the doors locked for fear of the Jewish leaders, Jesus came and stood among them and said, "Peace be with you!" After he said this, he showed them his hands and side. The disciples were overjoyed when they saw the Lord.
>
> Again, Jesus said, "Peace be with you! As the Father has sent me, I am sending you." And with that he breathed on them and said, "Receive the Holy Spirit."
>
> Now Thomas (also known as Didymus), one of the Twelve, was not with the disciples when Jesus came."

The apostles had abandoned Jesus in His darkest hour and bolted the doors in fear for their lives. Yet, nothing deterred Jesus from going after them. We might expect words of harsh reprimand and halted emotions. Instead, He extended peace, assurance, and grace. They received the breath of heaven and a bold commission.

And Thomas missed it all.

Where was he? One might hope he separated himself from the group to process his confusion in solitude. However, future verses indicate that he struggled to hold onto faith. The heavy burden of doubt and disappointment led to his intentional absence. Something in Thomas died alongside Jesus at the crucifixion. Now, in the crucible of his faith, Thomas withdrew from the others and isolated himself from those who saw Jesus. As hope faded, his mind reeled . . .

Weren't you the Messiah? How could this happen? I had been willing to die for you. I thought you had the authority to raise the dead. Now you are dead yourself! Who is going to lead us? Now, what is my purpose?

In the past, we might have been tempted to scratch our head at Thomas's absence and shake a scolding finger in his direction. But then, 2020 happened. Now, we have *all* experienced a season of unprecedented isolation and confusion. Through a pandemic, protests, and palpable fear, many of us felt crushed by situations outside of our control. We distanced ourselves socially and bolted ourselves behind closed doors. We grew weary from strains on marriages, finances, and education systems. We became depleted from demands on our physical, emotional, and mental health.

When we face a crisis of faith, the worst thing we can do is isolate ourselves from the community of other believers. When we do, like Thomas, we may miss the peace, the reassurance, and the empowerment we long for. Isolation is toxic for our souls. It gives Satan a dangerous opportunity to attack us from all sides. Instead, we need to surround ourselves with those who are looking for Jesus to show up.

Even when belief becomes suffocated by circumstances, Jesus never gives up on us. He is relentless in His pursuit. However, there is one door Jesus does not walk through uninvited. The doors of our hearts must be opened from the inside. We find the words of Jesus in Revelation chapter 3:20,

"Here I am! I stand at the door and knock. If anyone hears my voice and opens the door, I will come in and eat with that person, and they with me." He extends this invitation today. A life of peace and purpose is waiting for you. Unlock the door and let Jesus in.

A failure of trust doesn't have to define us. Anger doesn't have to control us. Disappointment doesn't have to derail us. Because Jesus overcame death and the grave in *His* darkest hours, we can believe that God's grace and strength will be enough in *ours*. In our final encounter between Thomas and Jesus, we will see a man pulled from loneliness and despair. As we do, we will find how Jesus also invites *us* to leave behind uncertainty and experience a life of unwavering faith.

Up Close with Hubert and Angela

As we wrestled with this chapter, it became hard to accept the picture of Thomas running from danger, deserting the Lord. How do you write a chapter on Thomas when he isn't in the story? However, we realized that Jesus did not expect him to confront His enemies. Jesus made it clear to the apostles that He must walk His path alone.

In the absence of the apostles, two things emerged for us: the significance of prophecy surrounding the events and the sudden appearance of people who found themselves being drawn to Jesus.

First, when Jesus submitted Himself to crucifixion, it became clear that prophetic voices described details hundreds of years earlier. Some Jewish scholars who witnessed the crucifixion knew immediately that they were seeing the fulfillment of prophecy. Now for us, prophecy fulfilled throughout Scripture provides us undeniable proof that Jesus appeared on the scene of human history as the Son of God, the Savior. We love the way Paul describes Jesus in Colossians 2:9, "In Christ all the fullness of the Deity lives in bodily form." He writes in 2 Corinthians

5:19, "God was in Christ, reconciling the world unto himself, not imputing their trespasses unto them." (KJV) That's why we love to call this the greatest love story ever told.

Second, we see people included in Jesus's story who were totally unexpected recipients of a close relationship with Jesus. One man, drawn from the crowd in Jerusalem, carried Jesus's cross. Another hung on his own cross beside the Lord. Two men who had stayed in the shadows during Jesus's three years of ministry now stepped forward front and center. And we can't help but wonder. Could the presence of Thomas and the apostles walking close to Jesus on the way to Golgotha have hindered a stranger from coming to know about Jesus? What if, as His most devoted followers, they started a riot and rushed Jesus down a secluded alley away from His destiny? What if the apostles had stood near the cross of Christ and made such loud cries that it drowned out the call of a dying sinner on a nearby cross? It may have kept him from entering the kingdom of heaven. If the apostles had buried the body of Jesus, two other men would have been denied the eternal reward God gave them for carefully caring for the body of Jesus and providing the place for His burial.

What does this tell us about God? The Bible says in 1 John 4:16, "God is love." It could have said, "God is power," as He possesses the greatest power in the universe. It could have said, "God is knowledge," as He contains all the knowledge in the universe. But instead, it says, "God is love." We trust that you have come to know this loving God better, and the way He has invited you into His story.

Come Closer

Takeaway
In the apostles' absence, God wrote all of humanity into this story.

1. God continually sought to prepare His people concerning future events about the coming Messiah through the message of the prophets of the Old Testament.
We included a handful of the several hundred prophecies concerning Jesus. How does the fulfillment of prophecy affect you?

2. Scripture is the way we know who God is and how we are included in His story. We are overwhelmed by His love to die for a stranger . . . for an enemy . . . for a criminal . . . and for those afraid to admit they followed Him.
This chapter expanded our understanding of the ways Jesus invites everyone closer. How does this help us to live as loved, to demonstrate His love to others, and lead them to become a part of God's story?

3. The heavy burden of doubt and disappointment led to his intentional absence. When we face a crisis of faith, the worst thing we can do is isolate ourselves from the community of other believers.

In what ways does isolation take a toll on our physical, mental, emotional, and spiritual health?

My prayer in my own words . . .

CHAPTER 9

Presence

Abandonment.
Rejection.
Isolation.
Doubt.

This list of words seems an unlikely precursor for one of the most impactful endings in all of Scripture. But God specializes in unlikely rescue stories. If He left it to *us* to write this episode for our season finale, we might have seen the last of Thomas. Perhaps we'd send Jesus searching for someone more dependable instead of someone who deserted Him. Maybe we'd decide Thomas proved himself untrustworthy and take resumes for a new apostle. Someone loyal . . . someone devoted . . . someone deserving.

Someone like us?

It's at this moment we remember the love of God. Grace is God's unmerited favor that gives us what we *don't* deserve, and mercy is God's provision that keeps us from getting what we *do* deserve. In John 20, we find the last and perhaps most poignant encounter between Thomas and Jesus. As the passage unfolds, we witness the beautiful conclusion to the story of a man broken by circumstances.

A Mission for the Missing

Jesus, in His great love and care for the apostles, wasted no time going to visit them on the evening of His resurrection. After He left them, finding Thomas became their primary order of business. They refused to let him simmer in self-imposed solitary confinement. John 20:25 says, "So the other disciples told him [Thomas], "We have seen the Lord!"

We see two types of people in this narrative: those who have drifted from faith and those who are determined to bring them home. Perhaps we have been both at some point in our lives. We may have isolated ourselves *from* others out of disappointment or misplaced hope. Left unchecked, disillusionment has led some to disengage from the church community and even deconstruct their faith. On the other hand, we may have been part of a search party *for* others. As followers of Christ, we have been given a mission to seek those that are missing. Whether we are a beginner believer or a seasoned leader, we are called to love those who are far from God or struggling in their faith. We are not responsible for the choices of others. However, we are charged by God with a mandate to pray, pursue, and point people to Him. We can ask the Holy Spirit for wisdom and discernment to guide our responses and reactions.

But if some of us were truly honest, we are tired. Tired as we watch someone we love drift further and further away from Jesus. Tired of tearful prayers and sleepless nights. Tired of waiting in silence and worried beyond our tipping point. Tired of faithfully sharing the gospel with seemingly little to show for it.

Satan doesn't care if our struggle is doubt or depletion; either can wear us down and weaken our resolve. We are called to carry the promise of a risen Savior, not the tattered fabric of a faded hope. When we are weighed down by a weary heart, we need the supernatural strength only Jesus can give. Before we share Jesus with others, we must first experience our own personal encounter with Him. He breathes new life into us to believe for impossible situations. His presence is the oxygen we desperately need.

That is what took place when Jesus appeared to the apostles. He breathed on them and told them to receive, or welcome, the Holy Spirit. Throughout the Old Testament, and until Jesus ascended to the Father, the Holy Spirit "came upon" people like prophets, prophetesses, judges, and kings. They spoke on behalf of God and accomplished seemingly impossible tasks through His power. Jesus knew this specific anointing of the Holy Spirit would give the apostles the encouragement to be brave enough to get out from behind locked doors and take their next steps.

Unless

The determined apostles pursued Thomas to join them again. When they told him they had seen Jesus alive, he could not bring himself to believe their words. John 20:25 says, "But he [Thomas] said to them, 'Unless I see the nail marks in his hands and put my finger where the nails were, and put my hand into his side, I will not believe.'"

Thomas the pragmatist wanted proof. Afraid to hope and depleted from disappointment, he sought an informed faith. He could not be content with hearsay or someone else's experience. Yet, beneath what might seem like a benign request lay a darker truth: Thomas doubted that Jesus had risen from the dead.

Thomas observed and walked with Jesus for three years. He knew Jesus as the Redeemer of those who had forfeited their souls to other things. He heard Jesus as the teacher who amazed all who listened to Him. He witnessed Jesus as the healer of the sick and watched with his own eyes as He raised Lazarus from the dead. *But that was then.*

To Thomas, Jesus bled to death on a cross and lay lifeless in a borrowed tomb. Despite their eyewitness account, his empty hope struggled to believe in an empty grave. He wrestled with so many questions. *Is this too good to be true? Will I be left with nothing but dashed hopes? And even if it is true, will Jesus still accept me when I have had these doubts about Him?*

Thomas needed more. He attached an *unless* to his willingness to believe. He asked for three things that seemed out of the realm of possibility:

- *Unless* I see the nail marks in His hands . . .
- *Unless* I put my finger where the nails were . . .
- *Unless* I put my hand into His side . . .

I will not believe.

Many people face the same dilemma that plagued Thomas. They hear firsthand accounts from those who have experienced true change after surrendering their life to Jesus. They read the records in the Bible of those who met with Jesus. And yet, they cannot bring themselves to believe that it can happen to them.

Sometimes, we don't want anyone to know we have doubts, so we tuck them away in silent spaces. Other times, we scream them—loud—so all the world can hear. We wrestle with so many questions: "God, are you good? Are you who you say you are? Where are you in this? How much longer will you let this go on? What if I trust you and it doesn't work out the way I hope? What am I supposed to do then?"

God welcomes our questions. His Word can stand up to the strongest of scrutiny. But unresolved doubt can lead to the deconstruction of our faith. Some of us, without even noticing, allowed our faith to erode through one word: *unless*. We may not have ever uttered the phrase aloud, but our belief systems have become so shattered that we don't know how to restart. We put God's character on trial when something didn't turn out like we thought it should. Or we withhold full confidence in God *until* something turns out like we think it should. We attach *unless* conditions to our willingness to believe.

- *Unless* I see relief from this pain in my life.
- *Unless* I finally get the answer I've been praying for.
- *Unless* I understand why this happened.

I will not believe.

Jesus already knows our *unless* places. He meets us there, but He doesn't want us to stay there. We don't have to be held hostage by deception or debilitated by doubt. We can invite the Holy Spirit to help us recognize anything that might be holding us back from complete surrender. When we do, He empowers us to come to grips with our doubts and grab hold of faith. Faith replaces the word *unless* with *regardless*.

"Regardless of the questions that remain unanswered in my life, I will not tether my faith to an outcome. I will stake my life on who Jesus says He is. I will believe."

We can be certain about one thing: this life will hold no shortage of uncertainties. Whether we are a seeker, a skeptic, or a seasoned leader, we must learn to manage the tension between doubt and faith. We must reconcile the reality of our pain and suffering with the truth that God is good. Only when we own our doubts can we truly own our faith. In *Fractured Faith: Finding Your Way Back to God in an Age of Deconstruction*, Lina AbuJamra writes, "Your present suffering is God's invitation to you for more of His presence in your life. . . . You will find that you are not alone in your pain, and that when you finally let it all out, God will still be right there, waiting for you. You will realize that God isn't disturbed by your pain. He welcomes it; He welcomes you. He's a Savior who is familiar with our pain. But He's also a Savior who knows that glory is born out of suffering."[1]

Just like we will see in the life of Thomas, we can accept Jesus's invitation to come closer no matter what tries to drive us away.

The Invitation

Perhaps Thomas began to realize what separation had come to cost him. John 20:26 says, "A week later his disciples were in the house again, and Thomas was with them." Drawn by the apostles, he found himself back in his community. Although we aren't privy to their conversations, their actions provide a template for relational discipleship. Rather than ostracize him, they opened the door and invited him in. If we find ourselves wrestling with doubt, we should never be afraid to return to a community of believers. Friend, don't miss out on the value of relationships. Lean into learning from others' knowledge and experience. Stay in the company of those who will cover you in prayer and go after God in worship. However, these requests sting if church hurt is what drove us away in the first place.

Our churches and small group settings need to be welcoming environments for those piecing together the fragments of their faith. Rather than shushing away doubt, church communities need to be leading healthy conversations that bring comfort and clarity. When our faith communities provide a safe space to process our questions, we are invited closer when doubt tries to drive us away.

Thomas's choice to return changed everything. He not only pushed past his internal struggle, but he also braved the danger of arrest. Gene A. Getz says, "They still kept the doors locked because hostility was mounting even more because of the incredible story that Jesus was no longer in the tomb. The religious leaders in Jerusalem were highly threatened, and to smoke-screen their own sins, they accused the Apostles of stealing Jesus' body and perpetuating a myth that He had risen from the dead."[2]

John 20:26 records the second time Jesus appeared to the apostles. "Though the doors were locked, Jesus came and stood among them and said, 'Peace be with you!'" Despite all that had happened, nothing kept Jesus from walking through locked doors, physically and spiritually, to unlock the potential in Thomas. In His first words, Jesus offered comfort and assurance to the anxious apostles. With intent, He scanned the room and narrowed his gaze to one person: Thomas.

That split second held a thousand words. What was this moment like for Thomas? Did he feel riddled with regret? Overwhelmed by grace? Or brokenhearted that he had missed the commission and the promise the others had received. Perhaps he averted his eyes, ashamed that he had left Jesus before the crucifixion. Or perhaps he looked straight ahead into the face of his risen Lord.

Jesus didn't wait for an apology or remind Thomas of his failure. Days earlier, Thomas had uttered a caustic challenge to his closest friends: "Unless . . ." Driven by despair, he had hit the bottom. Now, he and Jesus were face-to-face. Without hesitation, Jesus spoke these words of invitation: **"Put your finger here; see my hands. Reach out your hand and put it into my side"** (John 20:27).

Jesus knew exactly what Thomas needed. A crisis of faith had revealed his deepest doubt, but Jesus answered his deepest longing. Knowledge wasn't enough. Thomas needed to experience Jesus in a unique, personal way.

Not only did Thomas observe evidence of Jesus's resurrection, but he alone received an invitation to put his hands in Jesus's wounds. He accepted the truth that would set him free. He embraced the reassurance that would resolve the ache in his soul. He traded uncertainty for a life of resilient faith. Through Jesus, Thomas became brave enough to believe.

Please don't miss the order of Jesus's words. *First* came the invitation, **asking Thomas to come closer.** *Then* came the imperative: **"Stop doubting and believe"** (John 20:27). Jesus doesn't say, "Thomas, stop doubting, and then I'll let you get close to Me."

Before Jesus ever issued a command, He initiated restoration. Jesus didn't withdraw from Thomas, and He doesn't withdraw from us. We are not the sum total of our worst moments. We are known, wanted, and loved by the God who created us. No matter what we have done or what has been done to us, when we encounter Jesus, we are invited in. He doesn't want us to wait until we've figured it all out to move toward Him. He wants us to just keep showing up. He wants us to come closer even when we are still in the messy middle . . .

- In the middle of our confusion.
- In the middle of our questions.
- In the middle of our battle.
- In the middle of our uncertainty.

Because more than anything, we need an encounter with Jesus. *That's the secret.* We can come closer to Him in relationship through prayer and worship. His presence is the antidote to the poison of fear and doubt. We can face anything when we're facing it with Jesus. Even if it *feels* like He is distant, He never abandons us. Even if it *feels* like we can't hear Him, He is there. He wants us to get close enough to Him to understand His character accurately . . . close enough to His Word to know who He is . . . close enough to the awareness of His presence in our life that we know we are never alone. As we do, we learn how to walk by faith.

This became the turning point for Thomas. Completely convinced, all his questions and uncertainty dissipated in the presence of his risen Savior. With full surrender, Thomas exclaimed, "My Lord and my God!" (John 20:28). The original Greek literally reads, "The Lord of me and the God of me." Calling Him "Lord," Thomas used the word, *Kurios,* meaning "owner of my life." He invited Jesus to be in full control of his life and future.

That encounter forever marked Thomas. From this point on, he remained sold out for the kingdom of God. There is no record of him ever having another doubt about the presence and purpose Jesus had for him. Throughout Jesus's time with Thomas, He knew him as a man who had the courage to question and the bravery to believe. He knew Thomas would face intense persecution in days to come, and He prepared him to stand strong. He wanted Thomas to remember that He would be with him always, giving him the capacity to believe for even greater things. Through Thomas's example, others would place their faith in Jesus.

Faith Brings Blessing

Jesus marks our lives for kingdom purpose. We may still experience times when doubt tries to rear its ugly head, but it doesn't have to derail us. Jesus loves us too much to leave us in a state of doubt. The same command He issued to Thomas, He issues to us: "Stop doubting and believe" (John 20:27). As our relationship with Him grows, our doubts diminish. As we read His Word, our faith increases.

Romans 10:17 (KJV) says, "So then faith cometh by hearing, and hearing by the word of God." His Word provides the answers we need to overcome doubt and fulfill our God-given destiny. His Word gives us the firm foundation for faith that does not fail. In the appendix, we have included scripture verses to help trade doubts for God's truth and build a life of brave faith.

John 20:29–31 shares the conclusion of the encounter between Thomas and Jesus: "Then Jesus told him, 'Because you have seen me, you have believed.'" His next words addressed all to come, including our generation: "'Blessed are those who have not seen and yet have believed.' Jesus performed many other signs in the presence of his disciples, which are not recorded in this book. But these are written that you may believe that Jesus is the Messiah, the Son of God, and that by believing you may have life in his name." Unlike Thomas and the apostles, we cannot see Jesus here with us in bodily form. However, throughout this book, we have shared many reasons to put our faith in Him. When we do, we experience a life blessed by God.

We find both the definition and demonstration of faith in Hebrews 11:1–3, "Now faith is confidence in what we hope for and assurance about what we do not see. This is what the ancients were commended for. By faith we understand that the universe was formed at God's command, so that what is seen was not made out of what was visible." Verse 6 provides this important truth: "Without faith it is impossible to please God, because anyone who comes to him must believe that he exists and that he rewards those who earnestly seek him."

Brave faith believes that God exists and that He blesses those who put their trust in Him. Trust believes even when it cannot see. When we look at the Hall of Heroes in Hebrews chapter 11, we realize that they held strong in their faith without seeing all that had been promised to them. In verses 39–40 we read, "These were all commended for their faith, yet none of them received what had been promised, since God had planned something better for us so that only together with us would they be made perfect."

We may not receive the fulfillment of a promise in our lifetime. Yet, we can trust what God has planned. Only in eternity will we finally see the ways our faith linked arms with others who believed. There, with Thomas and those who fill the pages of Scripture, we will take our place. Until then, we leave a legacy of faith as we sow into the next generation.

Up Close with Angela

To my dad, Jim Argue was a brother-in-law and the closest of friends for more than fifty years. To me, he was an uncle, deeply admired and greatly loved. The life of Reverend Jim Argue was marked by a single phrase: "Faith is the unshakeable confidence in the character of God." This was never more tested than in the final years of his life.

God allowed me to witness a holy moment in the last week of my uncle's life. On one trip to Missouri to work with my dad on this book, we stopped by his home. As our family prayed and worshipped together, I thanked him and my Aunt Gloria for their faithfulness and example to us. I knew when I left it would be the last time I would see him alive. After many years of praying for healing this side of heaven, less than one week later, Jim was home.

His son, my cousin Randy Argue, shared this at his funeral:

The last seven years have been brutal on my father. I hated that his life was incrementally being taken by cancer. His teeth went first, yet his smile was bright. Next went his jawbone, then more jawbone, yet his attitude stayed positive. His ability to eat was taken, and finally, he couldn't even speak. His prayers were reduced to mumbles. It was hard to understand his words. But I told him that his prayers were probably more important than ever. To me, those mumbles sounded like a victory over his cruel circumstances. Suffering is so hard to understand. Dad stood strong . . . his faith did not waver.

It's hard to lose your hero and your dad on the same day. And yet, that's exactly what I was praying for on August 11, 2021. I was sitting on the tailgate of my truck, praying that God would end my dad's suffering. The sun was hot, then it disappeared behind the clouds that formed, and beams of sunlight began to shoot out across the valley floor. In that moment, God's Spirit spoke to me:

"Even when you can't see Me, I'm in control. I'm always working."

And that's when the suffering, the sadness, and even my questions, were all swallowed up in the overwhelming presence of God's love. Then the light show faded; the beams of sun diminished. I looked at the sky and asked out loud, "You took him, didn't You?" Just then, my mom sent a text that Dad was gone. I didn't even finish the text. My prayers were answered. I raised my arms and shouted like I was at a ball game: "You did it! You did it!"

My Uncle Jim lived a life of brave faith. We, too, are invited to get close enough to Jesus so that faith becomes the driving force of our lives. That's the place where "the suffering, the sadness, and even my [our] questions were [are] swallowed up in the overwhelming presence of God's love."

Up Close with Hubert

I decided at the age of eleven to seek God for His blessings. My Dad suggested that I memorize the first six verses of Psalm 1. I wrote the words on a 3 x 5 card and placed it on a shelf in my room where I would see it every day. As I began to memorize it, I made my choice: I would take God at His word. I believed God would bless me if I followed the instructions in Psalm 1.

Psalm 1:1–2 says,

> Blessed is the one
>   who does not walk in step with the wicked
> or stand in the way that sinners take
>   or sit in the company of mockers,
> but whose delight is in the law of the LORD,
>   and who meditates on his law day and night.

I saw these verses as a foundation for the blessings of God to be built upon in my life. I spent time each week meditating on God's Word and gaining an understanding of what it means to be blessed by God.

Blessing is defined as "God's favor and protection." It is further defined this way: "a beneficial thing for which one is grateful; something that brings well-being."[3] I saw in Genesis

12:1–4 how God used the words *bless* and *blessing* when He spoke to Abraham.

> Go from your country, your people and your father's household to the land I will show you.

> > I will make you into a great nation,
> > and I will bless you;
> > I will make your name great,
> > and you will be a blessing.
> > I will bless those who bless you,
> > and whoever curses you I will curse;
> > and all peoples on earth
> > will be blessed through you.

> So Abram went, as the Lord had told him.

I learned what God meant when He said to Abraham, "All peoples on earth will be blessed through you" (Genesis 12:3). This held the promise that Jesus would be born into the lineage of Abraham and people everywhere would be able to receive God's blessings through believing in Jesus.

Psalm 1:3 shares a metaphor for a person who is blessed by God.

> > That person is like a tree planted by streams of water,
> > > which yields its fruit in season
> > and whose leaf does not wither—
> > > whatever they do prospers.

I took this to be the evidence of the blessing—good health and prosperity, which I knew I wanted. I simply believed I had found God's provision for my life. I wanted to be a "blessed man."

Psalm 1:6 concludes by saying, "The LORD watches over the way of the righteous, but the way of the wicked leads to destruction." Here is our promise for the future: when we choose God's way, the blessings never end. I am so thankful that my dad cared enough to encourage me to memorize Psalm 1.

I am grateful for the blessings of the Lord—my wife and family that I enjoy so much, our friends where we pastored, my time as an administrator at Evangel University, and the financial provisions that have met our needs. Let's keep believing in Jesus and see His continued blessings come our way.

Come Closer

Takeaway
Come closer. . . . Stop doubting and believe

1. Some of us, without even noticing, allowed our faith to erode through one word: *unless*. Faith replaces the word *unless* with *regardless*.
Is there an *unless* in your life that needs to be replaced with *regardless*?

2. His Word provides the answers we need to overcome doubt and fulfill our God-given destiny. His Word gives us the firm foundation for faith that does not fail.
Later in "Trade Your Doubts for Brave Faith," we explore several potential doubts and God's answers. Which resonates most with you? Consider writing one of the verses below, keep it in a prominent place, and commit it to memory.

3. With full surrender, Thomas exclaimed, "My Lord and my God!" (John 20:28). The original Greek literally reads, "The Lord of me and the God of me." He invited Jesus to be in full control of his life and future.

How has this study of the life of Thomas impacted you and drawn you closer to Jesus?

My prayer in my own words . . .

CHAPTER 10

Future Unlimited

Jesus is alive.

Thomas is on the other side of his crisis of faith.

Our story is over, right?

Not even close.

Our story has only just begun.

Throughout this book, we highlighted four major encounters between Jesus and Thomas. We sat on the mountainside with Thomas as Jesus called him out of a crowd and appointed him to be an apostle. We witnessed the moment Thomas bravely spoke up and rallied the apostles to return to Bethany despite dangerous conditions. We leaned in as Thomas asked Jesus the hard questions about knowing the way to heaven. And we watched doubt and disappointment disappear as the scars of Jesus healed the wounds in him.

Although the Bible records no further conversations between Thomas and Jesus, he and the apostles continued to experience several encounters with Him after His resurrection. Jesus remained on the earth for another forty days, appearing to many and giving proof that He was alive.

We looked at two occasions where Jesus appeared to the apostles as they met behind locked doors. John 21 tells us that He appeared to them a third time by the Sea of Tiberias (Galilee). After a miraculous catch of fish, Peter realized it was the Lord and rushed to shore. Jesus engaged Peter in a conversation that restored him from the devastation of his denial and commissioned him to take care of His people.

In 1 Corinthians 15:3–8, the apostle Paul listed others who saw Jesus after His resurrection.

> For what I received I passed on to you as of first importance: that Christ died for our sins according to the Scriptures, that he was buried, that he was raised on the third day according to the Scriptures, and that he appeared to Cephas, and then to the Twelve. After that, he appeared to more than five hundred of the brothers and sisters at the same time, most of whom are still living, though some have fallen asleep. Then he appeared to James, then to all the apostles, and last of all he appeared to me also, as to one abnormally born.

During Jesus's final days on earth, He invited Thomas and the apostles to come closer once again to receive His last instructions.

Jesus's Parting Words and Ascension

Faithful to His mission, Jesus chose to spend His last moments with His closest followers, imparting crucial truths about their next steps. In Matthew 28:18–20, Jesus met them at a mountain and said to them, "All authority in heaven and on earth has been given to me. Therefore, go and make disciples of all nations, baptizing them in the name of the Father and of the Son and of the Holy Spirit, and teaching them to obey everything I have commanded you. And surely I am with you always, to the very end of the age."

Thomas sensed that Jesus's earthly ministry would soon come to a close, and he would soon lose sight of his greatest friend. However, he remembered earlier conversations when Jesus assured them that it would be to their advantage that He go so the Holy Spirit could come. They would never be alone.

Jesus would now be with them through the person of the Holy Spirit who would not only be *with* them but *in* them.

His disciples listened intently as Jesus explained the importance of why they were to wait for the Holy Spirit who would abide and dwell in them. In Acts 1:4–5 He told them, "Do not leave Jerusalem, but wait for the gift my Father promised, which you have heard me speak about. For John baptized with water, but in a few days you will be baptized with the Holy Spirit." When John the Baptist baptized Jesus in water, he told the people, "He [Jesus] will baptize you with the Holy Spirit and fire" (Matthew 3:11). Verse 8 of Acts continues, "But you will receive power when the Holy Spirit comes on you; and you will be my witnesses in Jerusalem, and in all Judea and Samaria, and to the ends of the earth."

The moment had come. Jesus lifted His hands and blessed them. While He blessed them, He ascended into heaven. In Acts 1:9–11 Luke writes, "A cloud hid him from their sight. They were looking intently up into the sky as he was going, when suddenly two men dressed in white stood beside them. 'Men of Galilee,' they said, 'why do you stand here looking into the sky? This same Jesus, who has been taken from you into heaven, will come back in the same way you have seen him go into heaven.'"

Just as when Jesus left the empty tomb, this final event to His earthly life is also marked by the appearance of two angels. On both occasions, they allowed themselves to be seen and heard. Their questions are telling. At the resurrection, they asked Mary, Jesus's mother, and Mary Magdalene, "Why do you look for the living among the dead? He is not here; He has risen!" (Luke 24:5–6). At the Ascension, they addressed Thomas and the apostles, "Why do you stand here looking into the sky?" (Acts 1:11), saying He will come back one day, like He went away.

Now, as we wait for His arrival, perhaps they would ask us, "Why are you looking for other things more than Jesus's return?" Scripture tells us that Jesus also has a question for our generation: "When the Son of Man returns, will he find faith on the earth?" (Luke 18:8). Jesus is looking for those who are brave enough to believe.

Mark 16:19 tells us where He is and what He is doing now. "After the Lord Jesus had spoken to them, he was taken up into heaven and he sat at the right hand of God." Paul writes in 1 Timothy 3:16, that He "was taken up in glory." The book of Hebrews shares that Jesus is the Mediator that reconciles mankind back to the Father. He saves those who come to God through Him and intercedes on their behalf. In a world racked by division and turmoil, His followers feel the effect of His love and care.

Hebrews 9:24, 28 state that He "appear[s] for us in God's presence" and "will appear a second time, not to bear sin, but to bring salvation to those who are waiting for Him." Jesus is active in a position of power and authority and will one day return as the King of Kings. Luke's Gospel tells us to be expectant because no one knows the day or the hour. Luke continues, "At that time they will see the Son of Man coming in a cloud with power and great glory. When these things begin to take place, stand up and lift up your heads, because your redemption is drawing near" (Luke 21:27–28). He will return to take every person who accepted Him as their Savior to live with Him for eternity. In a world of uncertainty, one thing is certain: Jesus lived, died, rose from the dead, and is coming again.

As Thomas and the apostles made their way toward Jerusalem, they reflected on everything they had seen and heard. They would soon be empowered by the Holy Spirit to effectively communicate the gospel of Jesus Christ everywhere they went.

The Promised Holy Spirit

Thomas chose to embrace the plan of God as it unfolded in his life. He trusted Jesus to do only what would be best for him. In obedience, he and the apostles soon arrived at the upper room.

Acts 2 tells us that a total of 120 followers of Jesus, including some women, gathered together there. Although none of them fully understood what the outpouring of the Holy Spirit would look like, they waited for the fulfillment of the promise.

After ten days, praying and worshipping God, Acts 2:1–4 says,

> When the day of Pentecost came, they were all together in one place. Suddenly a sound like the blowing of a violent wind came from heaven and filled the whole house where they were sitting. They saw what seemed to be tongues of fire that separated and came to rest on each of them. All of them were filled with the Holy Spirit and began to speak in other tongues as the Spirit enabled them.

This marked a new beginning for Thomas and the apostles. Their unity and willingness to wait ushered in the presence and power of the Holy Spirit. They would no longer lock themselves behind closed doors. Instead, they would carry the gospel to the far corners of the world—and it began at that very moment. We have no reason to think Thomas felt the least bit nervous or afraid to receive the fullness of the Holy Spirit. He believed Jesus's words recorded in John chapters 14–16:

- The Holy Spirit will be a Comforter and a Counselor to you. (John 14:26)
- "The Spirit of truth . . . lives with you and will be in you." (John 14:17)
- "The Advocate . . . will remind you of everything I have said to you." (John 14:26)
- "He will testify about me." (John 15:26)
- "He will glorify me." (John 16:14)

Thomas must have felt overwhelmed with excitement and awe as everything Jesus had promised now became an integral part of His life.

Acts 2:5–12 continues,

> Now there were staying in Jerusalem God-fearing Jews from every nation under heaven. When they heard this sound, a crowd came together in bewilderment, because each one heard their own language being spoken. Utterly amazed, they asked: "Aren't all these who are speaking Galileans? Then how is it that each of us hears them in our native language? Parthians, Medes and Elamites; residents of Mesopotamia, Judea and Cappadocia, Pontus and Asia, Phrygia and Pamphylia, Egypt and the parts of Libya near Cyrene; visitors from Rome, (both Jews and converts to Judaism); Cretans and Arabs—we hear them declaring the wonders of God in our own tongues!" Amazed and perplexed, they asked one another, "What does this mean?"

This was not a random day. God ordained this *particular* day when Jews who had been scattered all over the known world were present in Jerusalem to celebrate a festival. On the day of Pentecost, set aside as a harvest festival for the Jews, God poured out His Spirit in a way that ignited a "harvest of souls." People from various nations gathered outside the upper room as they heard the 120 speaking in their native languages. They knew these were languages Thomas and the others had never learned. This miraculous means of communication from God bore witness to the presence and power of His Spirit at work. It also confirmed the authenticity of the apostles' ministry that would soon follow. The gospel would no longer be confined to the Hebrew language. Now, the message of salvation through Jesus Christ would reach people of every nation.

Moments later, Peter stood and boldly addressed the crowd that had gathered, including some who had consented to the crucifixion of Jesus. Thomas watched in awe as God began to use his friend in a different way than he had ever seen before. Nothing would ever be the same. The remainder of Acts 2 shares Peter's riveting message. He told them that this supernatural event they were experiencing fulfilled God's plan, revealed to the prophet Joel hundreds of years before. Joel 2:28–29 says,

> I will pour out My Spirit on all people.
> Your sons and daughters will prophesy,
> your old men will dream dreams,
> your young men will see visions.
> Even on my servants, both men and women,
> I will pour out my Spirit in those days.

He also included the words from Joel 2:32, "Everyone who calls on the name of the LORD will be saved."

Peter reminded the crowd how they had witnessed the power of God in the ministry of Jesus. He told them they had put Jesus to death, with the help of the Romans, and that he had seen the resurrected Christ. When the crowd heard this, they were "cut to the heart," and they asked Peter and the other apostles, "Brothers, what shall we do?" (Acts 2:37). Peter replied, as written in verses 38–39, "Repent and be baptized, every one of you, in the name of Jesus Christ for the forgiveness of your sins. And you will receive the gift of the Holy Spirit. The promise is for you and your children and for all who are far off—for all whom the Lord our God will call."

The power of the Holy Spirit rested with such evidence on Peter's message that three thousand people immediately surrendered their lives to Christ. Thomas and the other apostles spent the entire day praying with people and baptizing them in water. This group formed the first church, meeting together and listening to the apostles' teaching. This glorious day marked the beginning of the first century church, a fellowship of Christians who would eventually bless the entire world.

Thomas and the others operated in power and boldness to bear witness to others about the resurrected Christ. However, they did this in the face of extreme opposition. The political and religious climate that surrounded Jesus's crucifixion and resurrection did not calm down. Persecution only intensified. Both the Jewish and Roman leaders wanted to stop the spread of the gospel message. The journey for Thomas and the apostles brought great gain for the kingdom of God. However, their commitment would eventually require their very lives.

Will our journey as a Christian always be easy? Like Thomas, we will experience times when the cost is great. We can be sure that God's love and grace will be sufficient for us in every circumstance. Romans 5:5 says, "And hope does not put us to shame, because God's love has been poured out into our hearts through the Holy Spirit, who has been given to us." In *Don't Miss Out: Daring to Believe Life Is Better with the Holy Spirit*, Jeannie Cunnion writes, "His Spirit is more proof of how much He loves us. It's evidence of how much He values us. You don't put your very Spirit in something that isn't immensely precious to you. And through the power of His Spirit in us, we can have more than a hopeful outlook in our suffering. We can supernaturally abound and prosper in hope."[1]

When we face what seem like impossible situations, we remember Paul's words in Ephesians 3:20–21, "Now to him who is able to do immeasurably more than all we ask or imagine, according to his power that is at work within us, to him be glory in the church and in Christ Jesus throughout all generations, for ever and ever! Amen."

As followers of Christ, we receive strength, comfort, and leadership through the person of the Holy Spirit. Romans 8:11 encourages us, "And if the Spirit of him who raised Jesus from the dead is living in you, he who raised Christ from the dead will also give life to your mortal bodies because of his Spirit who lives in you." Our strength can only go so far. Friend, we are completely dependent on the work of the Holy Spirit in us. There is so much more we could say about the Holy Spirit, and we encourage you to study Him on your own.

The Book of Acts

Thomas became a crucial part of each step of the apostles' ministry in Jerusalem and beyond. As we move forward in the book of Acts, we see him no longer as an unknown bystander from an unknown village. Thomas is no longer just a man being taught by the Master or a timid follower unsure of what he believed. Thomas moved forward as a confident leader who would soon be used by God to advance the gospel. He would make a lasting impact for Jesus among the people of other lands. But first, he and the apostles would have a powerful and effective ministry in and around Jerusalem.

As they shared the message of salvation through Jesus Christ, Acts chapter 5 tells us that many miraculous signs and wonders accompanied them. Verses 14–16 say:

> More and more men and women believed in the Lord and were added to their number. As a result, people brought the sick into the streets and laid them on beds and mats so that at least Peter's shadow might fall on some of them as he passed by. Crowds gathered also from the towns around Jerusalem, bringing their sick and those tormented by impure spirits, and all of them were healed.

God used Thomas in astounding ways to bring hope and healing to others. The man who once hesitated to believe now invited others to experience the miraculous and know Christ for themselves. As many people put their faith in Jesus, Thomas and the others faced harsh reactions from the Jewish hierarchy. Peter and John were arrested for preaching in the streets of Jerusalem and were put in prison overnight. Upon their release, they were commanded not to speak or teach in the name of Jesus. They could not obey this order. Instead, they bravely told the leaders that they must listen to God and tell about the things they had seen and heard from Jesus.

Thomas stayed involved in everything the apostles were doing. He helped to resolve conflicts that occurred in the early church established in Jerusalem. One is described in Acts 6:1–2: "The Hellenistic Jews among them complained against the Hebraic Jews because their widows were being overlooked in the daily distribution of food. So the Twelve [Apostles] gathered all the disciples together and said, 'It would not be right for us to neglect the ministry of the word of God in order to wait on tables.'" The apostles decided that seven men, known to be full of the Spirit and wisdom, should be chosen to provide care for the widows. Thomas and the other apostles laid their hands on the seven men and prayed that God would work through them mightily.

Acts 6 shares the tender story of one of the chosen seven. Verse 8 tells us, "Now Stephen, a man full of God's grace and power, performed great wonders and signs among the people." Some of the Jewish leaders began to argue with his teaching, but "they could not stand up against the wisdom the Spirit gave him as he spoke" (Acts 6:10). They raised false accusations against him and called him before the Sanhedrin.

After his powerful sermon, Acts 7:54–60 says,

> When the members of the Sanhedrin heard this, they were furious and gnashed their teeth at him. But Stephen, full of the Holy Spirit, looked up to heaven and saw the glory of God, and Jesus standing at the right hand of God. "Look," he said, "I see heaven open and the Son of Man standing at the right hand of God." At this they covered their ears and, yelling at the top of their voices, they all rushed at him, dragged him out of the city and began to stone him. Meanwhile, the witnesses laid their coats at the feet of a young man named Saul. While they were stoning him, Stephen prayed, "Lord Jesus, receive my spirit." Then he fell on his knees and cried out, "Lord, do not hold this sin against them." When he had said this, he fell asleep.

We can only imagine the heartbreak Thomas felt at the loss of a man he had helped to choose and commission. As a result of persecution, many believers scattered throughout Judea and Samaria. Even in the face of the danger of death, he and the apostles stayed in Jerusalem to oversee the church and resolve issues that arose. One such discussion involved Saul of Tarsus who gave the approval of the execution of Stephen.

Saul, whom we now know as the apostle Paul, lived as a devout Jewish leader who did not believe Jesus could be the Messiah. He persecuted Christians and sought to have them put to death because of their faith in Jesus Christ. Soon after Stephen's stoning, he made his way to Damascus to arrest believers and take them back to Jerusalem. Suddenly, he fell from his horse as he had a vision of the Lord. Jesus said to him, "Saul, Saul, why do you persecute me?" (Acts 9:4). Instantly struck with blindness, he received prayer from a man named Ananias. God restored his sight. In response to this miraculous encounter, Saul completely surrendered his life to Jesus and began to preach the gospel message in and around Damascus. Jewish leaders in the area began to conspire ways to have him killed. Saul the persecutor became Saul the persecuted.

Fellow believers led him by night to Jerusalem. They brought him to the apostles, who were initially reluctant to believe his conversion story. After hearing Saul's testimony of what happened in Damascus and his subsequent boldness to preach, Thomas and the apostles gave the approval of Saul to be an apostle. Thomas served an instrumental role in the onset of his ministry. Paul went on to evangelize many nations and write over a third of the New Testament.

Thomas and the apostles continued to be stretched in their leadership and understanding of what Jesus would expect of them. On the heels of Paul's conversion and acceptance, Peter found himself at the center of a conflict. He had a vision from

God in which God told him to go with three men to Caesarea. Upon arrival at the home of Cornelius, he preached about the death and resurrection of Jesus to a group of gentiles who immediately believed. Peter saw that God accepted not only Jews but gentiles and baptized them in water.

As word of their conversions reached the Jewish Christians in Jerusalem, Peter came under harsh criticism. Thomas and the apostles called a meeting and were stunned to hear his explanation. In Acts 11:15, 17 Peter shared, "As I began to speak, the Holy Spirit came on them as he had come on us at the beginning. Who was I to think that I could stand in God's way?" After the apostles discussed the matter, they had no further objections and praised God that He had granted even the gentiles repentance and salvation.

Through Paul, Peter, Thomas, and the other apostles, ministry expanded beyond Jerusalem to surrounding regions. Believers were added to the church daily and King Herod sought to stop the spread of the gospel. The inevitable happened. He arrested some of the believers and had the apostle James put to death. He also put Peter in prison with the intent to have him killed, but as the church prayed, God miraculously released Peter. Despite such extreme persecution, Acts 12:24 victoriously declares: **"But the word of God continued to spread and flourish."**

Thomas remained a part of crucial events and decisions that affected the course of the church and impacted generations to come. His story shows us how God can use anyone. The ordinary young man drawn from a crowd became a pillar of the early church. As an apostle, Thomas proved to be an influential leader, messenger, and "sent one," appointed by Jesus to preach the gospel of the kingdom.

The book of Acts has no *Amen* at the end, no closing. Today, the church is charged with the same mission and ministry entrusted to Thomas: take the gospel of Jesus Christ through the power of the Holy Spirit *until all have heard.*

The Future

God's assignment for Thomas took him to the subcontinent of India. This is confirmed through many historical records, even though his work there is not mentioned in the New Testament. We have included only a handful of the accounts we explored during our research.

Writer and museum curator Lucien de Guise writes,

> His least-used title is "Apostle of India." . . .
>
> When Vasco da Gama's fleet reached India in 1498, the Portuguese were surprised to find Christian communities thriving in the south of the Subcontinent. They were even more surprised by the locals' certainty that their church had been established by St. Thomas. They shouldn't have been, as countless travelers, including Marco Polo, had claimed that the saint's grave was there. . . .
>
> The evidence of Thomas's presence in India is considerable. . . .
>
> . . . Most of his bones were removed from India in the 3rd century and sent to Edessa in Mesopotamia, where the saint's vital role in India was acknowledged at the time.
>
> . . . In southern India, they still use the liturgical Syriac language—a dialect of the Aramaic language spoken by Jesus and St. Thomas. Syria was the bedrock of early Christianity. . . .
>
> At a time when the earliest Christian communities are being eradicated in the Middle East, their legacy at least lives on in India, thanks to St. Thomas.[2]

Thomas's work in India became notable and widespread. Numerous churches bear his name and represent a devoted following in India. Multiple sources confirm that Thomas died when killed by a spear on the Malayan Coast in India in AD 72. In *All the Apostles of the Bible*, Herbert Lockyer writes, "Thomas was . . . martyred by a lance thrust through his body while he was kneeling in prayer. A monument to his memory long continued to be shown at this spot. The Syrian Christians, settled on this coast centuries at least before European navigators reached India, claim Thomas as their founder."[3]

When Pope Benedict XVI visited India in 2006, he confirmed that Thomas had landed in western India, probably at a place that is part of present-day Pakistan. He then spread Christianity from there to southern India. It is said that Thomas was killed with a spear, and thus martyred in AD 72 in Mylapore, near Madras. The San Thome Basilica in Mylapore is situated at Thomas's tomb and was constructed by the Portuguese settlers in the 16th century.[4]

A population of Christians along the Malayan coast, on the western coast of India, credit their history of conversion to Thomas. Thomas's life and legacy lives on in India and in us. What he and those in the early church began, our generation continues to this day. Around the world, Christians are increasing in number. The global church is alive and well, a powerful expression of God's love to the lost, the downcast, the wounded, and the hurting. Best projections indicate that by 2030, every tribe, tongue, and nation will have received the message of the gospel in their language.

That means we are one day closer to the moment Jesus shared with Thomas and the apostles in John 14:1–4. His words offer the assurance we need in these uncertain times.

> Do not let your hearts be troubled. You believe in God; believe also in me. My Father's house has many rooms; if that were not so, would I have told you that I am going there to prepare a place for you? And if I go and prepare a place for you, I will come back and take you to be with me that you also may be where I am. You know the way to the place where I am going.

All that we know as temporary is fading. Jesus is coming. Heaven will be home for all who are brave enough to believe in Jesus Christ as their Lord and Savior. There, we will experience the ultimate encounter: we will see Him face-to-face. Revelation chapter 21:10, 14 tell us that we will also be able to see Thomas's name displayed in a significant place for all eternity. The apostle John writes, "He carried me away in the Spirit to a mountain great and high, and showed me the Holy City, Jerusalem, coming down out of heaven from God. The wall of the city had twelve foundations, **and on them were the names of the twelve apostles.**" And we, dear friends, will find our names written in the Lamb's Book of Life.

We pray that as you have come to know Thomas—the seeker, the skeptic, the sold-out follower, and the seasoned leader—you have been eternally changed by his story. Just as Jesus chose Thomas, He is choosing you. Just as God marked Thomas with kingdom purpose, God wants to use you.

As a conduit of grace to a broken world, you will bring light into dark places and hope into hurting hearts. You will be empowered by the Spirit to do what He calls you to do and go where He calls you to go. You can be bold . . . you can be fearless . . . you can be brave enough to believe.

Just as the early church advanced in times of persecution, the church of the living God is marching forward today. The gospel is still the power to save. Jesus is the same yesterday, today, and forever. We must anticipate His coming and invite all who will listen to be ready. We cannot choose silence and safety; we must choose obedience and opportunity.

We cannot shrink into the background or lock ourselves behind doors in fear. We cannot trade unwavering faith for an uncertain future. *We must be brave enough to believe.*

We cannot be afraid of persecution or resigned to irrelevance. We cannot be ashamed of accusation or relinquish our influence. *We must be brave enough to believe.*

We must be resolved to take Jesus to our Jerusalem—our homes, our schools, our cities, and our churches. *We must be brave enough to believe.*

We must be resolved to take Jesus to our Judea—our surrounding areas, our unsaved friends, and our nation. *We must be brave enough to believe.*

We must be resolved to take Jesus to Samaria—to those who feel marginalized and forgotten, those crippled by choices they regret, those too afraid or too bruised to step foot into a church. We must take Jesus to them. *We must be brave enough to believe.*

We must be resolved to take Jesus to the uttermost parts of the world—to the unreached who have not yet heard His name, to those in positions of power and authority, and to those in need of a Damascus Road encounter with Christ.

We can pray.

We can speak.

We can share.

We can go.

We can give.

We, dear friend, must be brave enough to believe.

Acknowledgments

Reverend Hubert Morris

Thank you to my wife, Glenda, for faithfully praying for me and patiently listening for many hours from other rooms in the house as I excitedly, often loudly, talked on the phone with Angela to write our words for this book.

Thanks to my dad, Hubert Morris Sr., and my mom, Sallie Morris, for influencing me and motivating me with their deep love for God's Word as I was growing up. I admired Dad's excellent preaching and Mom's faithfulness to teach the adult Bible class in her church until she was more than eighty years of age.

Google Docs has a whole new significance for me now, sitting in front of a computer, seeing Angela's words being typed, and her seeing my words being typed at the same time while talking on the phone together.

Thanks to our endorsers for their encouraging and supportive words. We are so grateful.

Reverend Angela Donadio

Thank you, Dad, for imparting your boundless love for God's Word and depth of insight about the life of Thomas into this labor of love. Writing this book with you is one of the most meaningful and significant experiences of my life. I'm grateful, not only for the faithful testimony you live, but for the legacy you leave through this book. What a gift this has been to me.

Thank you to my mom, Glenda Morris, who loves my father so well, loves her daughters and family so well, and the ways she raised us to love Jesus so well. Thank you for sharing my dad with me over countless phone calls and in-person visits as we worked on this book. Your fingerprints are found within these beloved pages.

Thank you to my extended family, my family in heaven, my River of Life Church family, and my friends close to home and around the world. Each one of you has impacted my life in profound ways.

My father and I both wish to thank the men and women who provided their gracious endorsement of this book on the life of Thomas. We admire your leadership and love for God and His Word. Thank you to our Iron Stream publishing family—Suzanne Kuhn, Larry J. Leech II, Bradley Isbell, and others who lent their time and talent to this project. Thank you also to Tawaan Brown for your creative genius and Keri Spring for your keen eye and treasured friendship.

Finally, thank you, Jesus. You know me better than anyone else and love me best.

APPENDIX

Trade Your Doubts for Brave Faith

I doubt that the Bible is truly the Word of God.
God's Answer:

- Matthew 24:35: "Heaven and earth will pass away, but my words will never pass away."
- 2 Timothy 3:16: "All Scripture is God-breathed and is useful for teaching, rebuking, correcting and training in righteousness."

I doubt that I am saved and ready to go to heaven when I die.
God's Answer:

- 1 Peter 1:8–9: "Though you have not seen him, you love him; and even though you do not see him now, you believe in him and are filled with an inexpressible and glorious joy, for you are receiving the end result of your faith, the salvation of your souls."
- Romans 10:9: "If you declare with your mouth, 'Jesus is Lord,' and believe in your heart that God raised him from the dead, you will be saved."
- Romans 10:13: "Everyone who calls on the name of the Lord will be saved."

- John 11:25–26: "Jesus said . . . 'I am the resurrection and the life. The one who believes in me will live, even though they die; and whoever lives by believing in me will never die. Do you believe this?'"

I doubt that God loves me.
God's Answer:

- John 3:16: "For God so loved the world that he gave his one and only Son, that whoever believes in him shall not perish but have eternal life."
- Romans 5:6–8: "You see, at just the right time, when we were still powerless, Christ died for the ungodly. Very rarely will anyone die for a righteous person, though for a good person someone might possibly dare to die. But God demonstrates his own love for us in this: While we were still sinners, Christ died for us."
- Romans 8:35–39: "Who shall separate us from the love of Christ? Shall trouble or hardship or persecution or famine or nakedness or danger or sword? As it is written: 'For your sake we face death all day long; we are considered as sheep to be slaughtered.' No, in all these things we are more than conquerors through him who loved us. For I am convinced that neither death nor life, neither angels nor demons, neither the present nor the future, nor any powers, neither height nor depth, nor anything else in all creation, will be able to separate us from the love of God that is in Christ Jesus our Lord."
- Ephesians 2:4–5: "But because of his great love for us, God, who is rich in mercy, made us alive with Christ even when we were dead in transgressions—it is by grace you have been saved."
- 1 John 3:1: "See what great love the Father has lavished on us, that we should be called children of God! And

that is what we are! The reason the world does not know us is that it did not know him."

I doubt that God can help my relationships improve.
God's Answer:

- Mark 11:24: "Whatever you ask for in prayer, believe that you have received it, and it will be yours." (If you have a Biblical promise for believing the answer is on the way, keep believing.)
- Hebrews 4:16: "Let us then approach God's throne of grace with confidence, so that we may receive mercy and find grace to help us in our time of need."
- James 1:6: "But when you ask, you must believe and not doubt, because the one who doubts is like a wave of the sea, blown and tossed by the wind."
- Hebrews 11:6: "Anyone who comes to him must believe that he exists and that he rewards those who earnestly seek him."
- Mark 9:23: Jesus said, "Everything is possible for one who believes."

I doubt that I can stop being depressed and discouraged every day.
God's Answer:

- Matthew 28:20: Jesus said, "Surely I am with you always, to the very end of the age."
- Philippians 4:6–7: "Do not be anxious about anything, but in every situation, by prayer and petition, with thanksgiving, present your requests to God. And the peace of God, which transcends all understanding, will guard your hearts and your minds in Christ Jesus."
- John 7:38–39: Jesus said, "Whoever believes in me, as Scripture has said, rivers of living water will flow from

within them. By this he meant the Spirit, whom those who believed in him were later to receive. Up to that time the Spirit had not been given, since Jesus had not yet been glorified." Ephesians 5:18 continues, "Be filled with the Spirit."

- Isaiah 25:1:

> Lord, you are my God;
>   I will exalt you and praise your name,
> for in perfect faithfulness
>   you have done wonderful things,
>   things planned long ago.

I doubt that God can heal me.
God's Answer:

- 1 Peter 2:24: "'He himself bore our sins' in his body on the cross, so that we might die to sins and live to righteousness; 'by his wounds you have been healed.'"
- James 5:14–15: "Is anyone among you sick? Let them call the elders of the church to pray over them and anoint them with oil in the name of the Lord. And the prayer offered in faith will make the sick person well; the Lord will raise them up. If they have sinned, they will be forgiven."
- Jeremiah 30:17:

> "But I will restore you to health
>   and heal your wounds,"
> declares the Lord.

- Exodus 23:25: "Worship the Lord your God, and his blessing will be on your food and water. I will take away sickness from among you."
- Proverbs 4:20–22:

> Pay attention to what I say;
>   turn your ear to my words.

> Do not let them out of your sight,
>> keep them within your heart;
> for they are life to those who find them
>> and health to one's whole body.

- James 5:16: "Therefore confess your sins to each other and pray for each other so that you may be healed. The prayer of a righteous person is powerful and effective."

I doubt God has a plan for my life and my future.
God's Answer:

- Jeremiah 1:5:

  > Before I formed you in the womb I knew you,
  >> before you were born I set you apart;
  > I appointed you a prophet to the nations.

- Jeremiah 29:11: "'For I know the plans I have for you,' declares the LORD, 'plans to prosper you and not to harm you, plans to give you hope and a future.'"
- Esther 4:14: "You have come to your royal position for such a time as this?"
- Romans 8:28: "And we know that in all things God works for the good of those who love him, who have been called according to his purpose."
- Psalm 33:11: "The plans of the LORD stand firm forever, the purposes of his heart through all generations."
- Proverbs 3:5–6:

  > Trust in the LORD with all your heart
  >> and lean not on your own understanding;
  > in all your ways submit to him,
  >> and he will make your paths straight.

Doubt destabilizes. . . . Faith makes you solid.
Doubt delays your decisions. . . . Faith frames your decisions.
Doubt weakens our ability to persevere under trial. . . . Faith
brings strength and sets us free to make progress.
Doubt brings confusion. . . . Faith brings confidence.
"For we live by faith, not by sight." (2 Corinthians 5:7)

Notes

2. Called Out of the Crowd

1. Britannica, s.v. "apostle," https://www.britannica.com/topic/Apostle.

2. Oswald Chambers, *My Utmost for His Highest*, Updated Edition, ed. James Reimann (Grand Rapids, MI: Discovery House, 1992), October 17.

3. Jessie Seneca, "Walk in Your Calling with Leadership Trainer Jessie Seneca," December 29, 2020, in *Make Life Matter*, interview by Angela Donadio, podcast, MP3 audio, 40:01, https://kingdomwinds.com/podcast/make-life-matter-walk-in-your-calling-with-leadership-trainer-jessie-seneca-2/.

4. Mark Ballenger, "3 Differences Between God's Voice and the Voice in Your Head, ," Apply God's Word, January 20, 2019, https://applygodsword.com/3-differences-between-gods-voice-and-the-voice-in-your-head/.

5. Paula Faris, "Former Host of 'The View' Paula Faris—Called Out," August 20, 2020, in *Greenelines*, interview by Steve Greene, podcast, MP3 audio, 36:23, https://greenelines.libsyn.

com/former-host-of-the-view-paula-faris-called-out-season-6-ep-151.

6. Dr. Naomi Dowdy, *Moving On and Moving Up* (Dallas: Naomi Dowdy Ministries, 2012).

7. Jackie Hill Perry, "A Deep Talk About Holiness," April 15, 2021, in *Made for This with Jennie Allen*, podcast, MP3 audio, 25:33, https://www.spreaker.com/user/jennieallen/s7-ep22-jackie-hill-perry-fc.

3. Awakened to Purpose

1. Harmony Klingenmeyer, "Called to Do Hard Things," June 22, 2021, in *Make Life Matter*, interview by Angela Donadio, podcast, MP3 audio, 40:58, https://kingdomwinds.com/podcast/make-life-matter-called-to-do-hard-things-with-harmony-klingenmeyer/.

2. Mike Todd, "Playing It Safe? This Is for You," October 7, 2021, in *Made for This with Jennie Allen*, podcast, MP3 audio, 38:02, https://www.spreaker.com/user/jennieallen/s9-ep6-mike-todd-fc.

3. Bethany Marshall, "Rooted Deep in the Wait," June 1, 2021, in *Make Life Matter*, interview with Angela Donadio, podcast, MP3 audio, 36:48, https://kingdomwinds.com/podcast/make-life-matter-rooted-deep-in-the-wait-with-bethany-marshall/.

4. Hal Donaldson, "Hope That Changes Lives," May 3, 2021, in *Make Life Matter*, interview by Angela Donadio, podcast, MP3 audio, 33:07, https://kingdomwinds.com/podcast/make-life-matter-disruptive-compassion-convoy-of-hope-with-hal-donaldson/.

4. A Setup

1. Google definitions, s.v. "glory," from Oxford Languages.

2. Tara-Leigh Cobble, *The Bible Recap: A One-Year Guide to Reading and Understanding the Entire Bible* (Bloomington, MN: Bethany House, 2020).

5. A Step-Up

1. Herbert Lockyer, *All the Apostles of the Bible* (Grand Rapids: Zondervan, 1988), 177.

2. Jon Tyson, *Beautiful Resistance: The Joy of Conviction in a Culture of Compromise* (Multnomah, 2016), 104.

3. Caroline Leaf, *Switch on Your Brain: The Key to Peak Happiness, Thinking, and Health* (Grand Rapids: Baker Books, 2015), 38, 53.

4. Jan Aldridge, "Miraculously Healed," September 27, 2021, in *Make Life Matter*, interview by Angela Donadio, podcast, MP3 audio, 40:58, https://kingdomwinds.com/podcast/make-life-matter-miraculously-healed-with-jan-aldridge/.

5. Gracia Burnham, "In the Presence of My Enemies," April 20, 2021, in *Make Life Matter*, interview by Angela Donadio, podcast, MP3 audio, 43:30, https://kingdomwinds.com/podcast/make-life-matter-in-the-presence-of-my-enemies-with-gracia-burnham/.

6. Jennifer Rothschild, "Live Beyond Limits," March 2021, in *Make Life Matter*, interview by Angela Donadio, podcast, MP3 audio, 29:51, https://kingdomwinds.com/podcast/make-life-matter-live-beyond-limits-with-jennifer-rothschild/.

7. Lisa Whittle, *The Hard Good: Showing Up for God to Work in You When You Want to Shut Down* (Nashville: Thomas Nelson, 2021), 176, 184.

6. The Place

1. "Multi-Lingual Ma Nishtana (Four Questions)," Chabad. org, https://www.chabad.org/holidays/passover/pesach_cdo/ aid/411719/jewish/Multi-Lingual-Ma-Nishtana-Four-Questions.htm.

2. Billy Graham, *Where I Am: Heaven, Eternity, and Our Life Beyond* (Nashville: Thomas Nelson, 2015).

3. A. W. Tozer, *Tozer for the Christian Leader: A 365-Day Devotional* (Chicago: Moody Publishers, 2015), 17.

4. Alisa Childers, *Another Gospel?: A Lifelong Christian Seeks Truth in Response to Progressive Christianity* (Carol Stream, IL: Tyndale Momentum, 2020), 200.

5. Angela Donadio, *Astounded: Encountering God in Everyday Moments* (Alachua, FL: Bridge-Logos, Inc., 2020), 34.

7. The Way

1. Dustin Crowe, "The 7 'I AM' Statements of Jesus: OT Background and NT Meaning," *Indycrowe* (blog), February 13, 2019, https://indycrowe.com/2019/02/13/the-7-i-am-statements-of-jesus-ot-background-nt-meaning/.

2. Gene Getz, *The Apostles: Becoming Unified Through Diversity (Men of Character)* (Nashville: B&H Books, 1998), 139.

3. "George Barna," Barna, https://www.barna.com/about/george-barna/.

4. George Barna, "God's Truth or My Truth?" August 29, 2021, in *Make Life Matter*, interview by Angela Donadio, podcast, MP3 audio, 40:58, https://kingdomwinds.com/podcast/make-life-matter-gods-truth-or-my-truth-with-dr-george-barna/.

8. Absence

1. "How Many Prophecies Did Jesus Fulfill?" Got Questions, https://www.gotquestions.org/prophecies-of-Jesus.html.

2. "What Is Worship? Proskuneo," Worship Arts Conservatory, December 10, 2015, https://www.worshiparts.net/what-is-worship-proskuneo/. See also James Strong, *New Strong's Exhaustive Concordance*, s.v. "proskuneo" (Nashville: Thomas Nelson, 2003).

9. Presence

1. Lina AbuJamra, *Fractured Faith: Finding Your Way Back to God in an Age of Deconstruction* (Chicago: Moody Publishers, 2021), 36.

2. Gene Getz, *The Apostles: Becoming Unified Through Diversity (Men of Character)* (Nashville: B&H Books, 1998), 142.
3. Google definitions, s.v. "blessing," from Oxford Languages.

10. Future Unlimited

1. Jeannie Cunnion, *Don't Miss Out: Daring to Believe Life Is Better with the Holy Spirit* (Bloomington, MN: Bethany House, 2021), 40–41.

2. Lucien de Guise, "The little-known story of how St. Thomas the Apostle brought Christianity to India," Aleteia, May 18, 2018, https://aleteia.org/2018/05/18/the-little-known-story-of-how-st-thomas-the-apostle-brought-christianity-to-india/.

3. Herbert Lockyer, *All the Apostles of the Bible* (Grand Rapids: Zondervan, 1988), 260.

4. "Thomas the Apostle," The Famous People, https://www.thefamouspeople.com/profiles/thomas-the-apostle-37216.php.